Samuel Hart Wright, Society American Tract

The Illustrated Family Christian Almanac for the United

States

for the year of our Lord and Saviour Jesus Christ, 1867

Samuel Hart Wright, Society American Tract

The Illustrated Family Christian Almanac for the United States
for the year of our Lord and Saviour Jesus Christ, 1867

ISBN/EAN: 9783337314743

Printed in Europe, USA, Canada, Australia, Japan

Cover: Foto ©Lupo / pixelio.de

More available books at **www.hansebooks.com**

THE ILLUSTRATED

Family Christian Almanac

FOR

THE UNITED STATES,

FOR· THE

YEAR OF OUR LORD AND SAVIOUR JESUS CHRIST

1867,

BEING THE THIRD AFTER BISSEXTILE, AND UNTIL JULY 4TH, THE 91ST YEAR
OF THE INDEPENDENCE OF THE UNITED STATES.

CALCULATED FOR

BOSTON, NEW YORK, WASHINGTON, AND CHARLESTON,

AND

FOUR PARALLELS OF LATITUDE.

ADAPTED FOR USE THROUGHOUT THE COUNTRY.

WITH

VALUABLE SCIENTIFIC AND USEFUL INFORMATION.

ASTRONOMICAL CALCULATIONS, IN EQUAL OR CLOCK TIME,

BY DR. SAMUEL HART WRIGHT, A. M.

PENN YAN, YATES COUNTY, NEW YORK.

BOSTON, Lat. 42° 21′ N.; Long. 71° 4′ W.
NEW YORK, Lat. 40° 42′ 40″ N.; Long. 74° 1′ W
WASHINGTON, Lat. 38° 53′ N.; Long. 77° W.
CHARLESTON, Lat. 32° 47′ N.; Long. 79° 57′ W.

PUBLISHED BY THE

AMERICAN TRACT SOCIETY,

150 NASSAU-STREET. NEW YORK,

AND SOLD BY BOOKSELLERS AND TRADERS.

☞ Entered according to Act of Congress, in the year 1866, by O. R. Kingsbury, in the Clerk's Office of the District Court for the Southern District of New York.

CONJUNCTION OF THE PLANETS, AND OTHER PHENOMENA.

Month.	Aspect.	Time. D.	H.	M.	Distance apart.	°	′
Jan	☽ near ♀	3	0	30 m.	♀	0	5 S.
	☽ near ♃	7	6	34 e.	♃	4	25 S.
	♂ ☍ ☉	10	3	51 e.	♂	180	0
	☽ near ♂	19	7	34 m	♂	8	58 N.
	☽ near ♄	28	4	22 e.	♄	2	14 S.
	☽ near ♀	31	0	54 e	♀	0	29 S.
Feb.	♃ ☌ ☉	3	0	55 e.		0	0
	♃ near ☿	7	3	56 m	☿	1	30 S.
	♄ □ ☉	12	5	29 e.	♄	90	0 W.
	☽ near ♂	15	6	36 m.	♂	8	44 N.
	♂ stationary	18	5	22 e.			
	♀ gr. elon. W.	20	5	28 m.	♀	46	48 W.
	☽ near ♄	25	2	23 m.	♄	2	15 S.
Mar.	☽ near ♀	2	6	28 m.	♀	2	12 S.
	♄ stationary	4	4	47 m			
	☽ near ♃	4	10	21 m.	♃	3	36 S.
	☽ near ☿	7	1	2 e	☿	2	38 N.
	☿ gr. elon. E.	9	9	35 e.	☿	18	19 E.
	☽ near ♂	14	6	29 e.	♂	7	54 N.
	☽ near ♄	24	10	26 m.	♄	2	15 S.
	♀ near ♃	31	3	32 e.	♀	0	41 N.
April	☽ near ♃	1	6	46 m.	♃	3	10 S.
	☽ near ♀	1	7	59 m.	♀	2	26 S.
	☽ near ♂	11	4	27 e.	♂	6	56 N.
	♂ □ ☉	15	6	24 e.	♂	90	0 W.
	☽ near ♄	20	3	28 e.	♄	2	4 S.
	☿ gr. elon. W.	22	10	35 e.	☿	27	13 W.
	☽ near ♃	29	1	15 m.	♃	2	42 S.
May	☽ near ♀	1	7	39 m.	♀	0	40 S.
	☽ near ♂	9	8	34 e.	♂	5	28 N.
	♄ ☍ ☉	11	7	37 e.	♄	180	0
	☽ near ♄	17	6	20 e.	♄	1	56 S.
	☽ near ♃	26	3	55 e.	♃	2	17 S.
	♃ □ ☉	27	5	40 e.	♃	90	0 W.
	☽ near ♀	31	4	18 m.	♀	2	3 N.
June	☽ near ♂	7	5	16 m.	♂	3	47 N.
	☽ near ♄	13	8	32 e.	♄	2	0 S.
	☽ near ♃	23	1	17 m.	♃	2	1 S.
	♃ stationary	27	10	7 m.			
	☽ near ♀	30	0	42 m.	♀	4	9 N.
July	☽ near ☿	3	2	15 e.	☿	3	34 N.
	☽ near ♂	5	4	46 e.	♂	1	48 N.
	☿ gr. elon. E.	6	3	4 m.	☿	26	11 E.
	☽ near ♄	11	0	26 m.	♄	2	15 S.
July	☽ near ♃	20	5	20 m.	♃	2	3 S.
	♄ stationary	22	5	23 e.			
	☽ near ♀	29	10	20 e.	♀	4	33 N.
Aug.	☽ near ♂	3	6	56 m.	♂	0	21 S.
	☽ near ♄	7	7	24 m.	♄	2	39 S.
	♀ near ☿	10	7	6 m.	☿	4	37 S.
	♄ □ ☉	10	5	19 e.	♄	90	0 E.
	☽ near ♃	16	5	59 m.	♃	2	20 S.
	☿ gr. elon. W.	21	2	4 m.	☿	18	27 W.
	♃ ☍ ☉	26	2	17 m.	♃	180	0
	☽ near ♀	28	8	25 e.	♀	2	53 N.
	☽ near ♂	31	11	37 e.	♂	2	22 S.
Sept.	☽ near ♄	3	5	49 e.	♄	2	49 S.
	♀ near ☿	10	3	48 e.	☿	0	22 N.
	☽ near ♃	12	6	45 m.	♃	2	42 S.
	♀ sup. ☌ ☉	25	11	10 m.		0	0
	☽ near ♂	29	8	2 e.	♂	4	7 S.
Oct.	☽ near ♄	1	7	1 m.	♄	2	57 S.
	☽ near ♃	9	10	49 m.	♃	2	49 S.
	♂ near ☿	19	5	36 e.	☿	1	55 S.
	♃ stationary	24	9	9 m.			
	♄ near ☿	25	9	47 e.	☿	4	45 S.
	☽ near ♀	27	10	32 e.	♀	4	0 S.
	☽ near ♂	28	5	30 e.	♂	5	13 S.
	☽ near ♄	28	9	14 e.	♄	2	59 S.
	☽ near ☿	29	4	7 m.	☿	7	52 S.
	☿ gr. elon E.	31	6	33 e.	☿	23	39 E.
Nov.	☽ near ♃	5	7	23 e.	♃	2	35 S.
	♄ near ♀	7	8	18 m.	♀	1	49 S.
	♂ near ♀	14	6	37 e.	♀	0	21 N.
	♀ near ☿	15	3	35 e.	☿	1	8 S.
	♂ near ☿	15	11	2 e.	☿	0	43 S.
	♄ ☌ ☉	19	6	36 m.		0	0
	♃ □ ☉	21	1	11 e.	♃	90	0 E.
	☽ near ♄	25	10	55 m.	♄	3	4 S.
	☽ near ♂	26	7	2 e.	♂	5	37 S.
	☽ near ♀	27	9	15 m.	♀	5	38 S.
Dec.	☽ near ♃	3	7	46 m.	♃	2	0 S.
	☿ gr. elon. W.	9	1	0 e.	☿	21	0 W.
	♄ near ☿	12	7	29 m.	☿	0	9 N.
	☽ near ♄	22	11	16 e.	♄	3	16 S.
	☽ near ♀	27	11	41 e.	♀	4	43 S.
	☽ near ♃	30	10	44 e.	♃	1	18 S.

CHARACTERS EXPLAINED.—☿ Mercury, ♀ Venus, ♂ Mars, ♃ Jupiter, ♄ Saturn, ☽ Moon, ☉ Sun, ☍ opposition or half a circle apart, □ quadrature or quarter of a circle apart, ☌ conjunction or together, having the same *right ascension*; the word *near* used above means the same, and indicates that the two bodies are then on a line running from the North Pole through both; gr. elon., greatest elongation or farthest distance from the Sun; stationary, when the planet is without apparent motion, and is about to move in a direction contrary to that it last had. The above table enables us to find the planets throughout the year.

ECLIPSES FOR THE YEAR 1867.

There will be two eclipses of the Sun and two of the Moon.

I. An annular eclipse of the Sun, March 6. Invisible in America, but visible in Europe, Africa, and Asia. See the map of this eclipse.

II. A partial eclipse of the Moon early in the morning of Wednesday, March 20. Visible throughout America. In California and Oregon it will begin in the evening of the 19th. For the points of first and last contact with the shadow, and the direction of the Moon's path through it, see the engraving of this eclipse. For the times of its phases, see annexed table.

III. A total eclipse of the Sun, August 29. Invisible in the United States, but visible in South America. See the map of this eclipse.

IV. A partial eclipse of the Moon, Friday evening, September 13. Visible in America generally. This eclipse will begin before the Moon rises at places west of Boston, and it will therefore rise more or less eclipsed. In the Pacific states this eclipse is wholly invisible. For the points of first and last contact with the Earth's shadow, and the direction of the Moon's track through it, see the engraving of this eclipse. For the times of the several phases, see the annexed table.

Principal places.	Eclipse of March 20. Begins, morn.	Eclipse of March 20. Ends, morn.	Eclipse of Sept. 13. Begins, eve.	Eclipse of Sept. 13. Ends, eve.	Principal places.	Eclipse of March 20. Begins, morn.	Eclipse of March 20. Ends, morn.	Eclipse of Sept. 13. Begins, morn.	Eclipse of Sept. 13. Ends, eve.
	H. M.	H. M.	H. M.	H. M.		H. M.	H. M.	H. M.	H. M.
Halifax, N. S.	3 1	6 8	6 43	9 42	Augusta, Ga.	1 48	4 55		8 29
Eastport, Me.	2 46	5 53	6 28	9 27	Cleveland, Ohio	1 47	4 54		8 28
Bangor, Me.	2 39	5 46	6 21	9 20	Havana, Cuba	1 46	4 53		8 27
Augusta, Me.	2 36	5 43	6 18	9 17	Detroit, Mich.	1 43	4 50		8 24
Brunswick, Me.					Columbus, Ohio				
Portland, Me.	2 34	5 41	6 16	9 15	Cincinnati, Ohio				
Boston, Mass.	2 31	5 38	6 13	9 12	Lansing, Mich.	1 38	4 45		8 19
Cambridge, Mass.					Lexington, Ky.				
Quebec, C. E.					Tallahassee, Fla.	1 37	4 44		8 18
Providence, R. I.	2 30	5 37		9 11	Frankfort, Ky.				
Lowell, Mass.					Fort Wayne, Ind.	1 34	4 41		8 15
Newport, R. I.					Louisville, Ky.	1 34	4 40		8 14
Concord, N. H.	2 29	5 36		9 10	Indianapolis, Ind.	1 31	4 38		8 12
Montpelier, Vt.					Grand Haven, Mich.	1 29	4 36		8 10
Hartford, Conn.	2 25	5 32		9 6	Nashville, Tenn.	1 28	4 35		8 9
Springfield, Mass.					Chicago, Ill.	1 25	4 32		8 6
Northampton, "	2	5 30		9 4	Evansville, Ind.				
New Haven, Conn.					Tuscaloosa, Ala.	1 24	4 31		8 5
Montreal, C. E.	2 21	5 28		9 2	Milwaukie, Wis.	1 22	4 29		8 3
Troy, N. Y.					Mobile, Ala.				
Albany, N. Y.	2 20	5 27		9 1	Cairo, Ill.				
Hudson, N. Y.					Hickman, Ky.	1 17	4 24		7 58
New York					Madison, Wis.				
Schenectady, N.Y.					Springfield, Ill.				
Newburg, N. Y.	2 19	5 26		9 0	New Orleans, La.	1 15	4 22		7 56
Po'keepsie, N. Y.					Jackson, Miss.				
Trenton, N. J.	2 17	5 24		8 58	St. Louis, Mo.	1 14	4 21		7 55
Philadelphia, Pa.	2 15	5 22		8 56	Galena, Ill.				
Utica, N. Y.					Dubuque, Iowa	1 12	4 19		7 53
Ogdensburg, N. Y.	2 12	5 19		8 53	La Crosse, Wis.				
Wilmington, Del.					Natchez, Miss.	1 10	4 17		7 51
Baltimore, Md.					Baton Rouge, La.				
Auburn, N. Y.	2 9	5 16		8 50	Keokuk, Iowa				
Annapolis, Md.					Quincy. Ill.	1 8	4 15		7 49
Harrisburg, Pa.	2 8	5 15		8 49	Iowa City, Iowa				
Kingston, C. W.					Jefferson City, Mo.	1 7	4 14		7 48
Washington, D. C.					Little Rock, Ark.	1 6	4 13		7 47
Penn Yan, N. Y.	2 7	5 14		8 48	Superior City, Wis.	0 59	4 6		7 40
Geneva, N. Y.					Des Moines, Iowa				
Canandaigua, N.Y.					St. Paul, Minn.				
Frederickton, Va.	2 6	5 13		8 47	St. Joseph, Mo.	0 55	4 2		7 36
Petersburg, Va.					Lawrence, Kansas	0 53	4 0		7 34
Richmond, Va.	2 5	5 12		8 46	Omaha City, Neb.	0 51	3 58		7 32
Rochester, N. Y.	2 4	5 11		8 45	Vera Cruz, Mex.				
Buffalo, N. Y.	2 0	5 7		8 41	Matamoros, Mex.	0 44	3 51		7 25
Raleigh, N. C.					Austin, Texas				
Toronto, C. W.					Mexico	0 39	3 46		7 20
Georgetown, S. C.	1 58	5 5		8 39	Santa Fé, N. M.	0 11	3 18		6 52
Panama, N. G.					Salt Lake City, Utah	11 46	2 53		6 27
Pittsburg, Pa.					Oregon City, Or.	11 11	2 18		
Charleston, S. C.	1 56	5 2		8 36	Sacramento City, Cal.	11 8	2 15		
Chagres, N. G.					Monterey, Cal.	11 7	2 14		
Erie, Pa.	1 55	5 0		8 34	Portland, Or.	11 5	2 12		invisible.
Wheeling, W. Va.					San Francisco, Cal.				
Savannah, Ga.	1 51	4 58		8 32	Salem, Or.	11 2	2 9		
Columbia, S. C.					Astoria, Or.	11 0	2 7		
St. Augustine, Fla.	1 49	4 56		8 30	Neeah, Wash. Ter.	10 56	2 3		

THE SEASONS.

				R. M.			D.	H.	M.
Winter	begins	December	21, 1866	..7	42 eve., and lasts	..	89	0	48
Spring	"	March	20, 1867	..8	30 eve.,	"	..92	20	34
Summer	"	June	21, 1867	..5	4 eve.,	"	..93	11	23
Autumn	"	September	23, 1867	..7	27 mo.,	"	..89	18	4
Winter	"	December	22, 1867	..1	3¼ mo. Trop.year, 365			5	49

MORNING AND EVENING STARS.

VENUS will be Morning Star until September 25, when it is in superior conjunction with the Sun, being then rendered invisible by the superior light of the Sun; and being also at its maximum distance from the Earth, it will have its minimum apparent diameter, and its disc, if visible, will be a perfect circle. After this date it will soon appear low in the west soon after sunset, being Evening Star, and daily appearing further east of the Sun. At the close of the year 1866 it shows beautifully as a Morning Star, increasing in splendor until January 17, when its illuminated disc is greatest. It rises then about 4h. 23m. mo. On February 24 it reaches its greatest elongation—46° 48'—west of the Sun, whence it moves off towards the Sun and superior conjunction, with daily decreasing light. On January 1, it will be north-east of Antares; on February 5, it enters Sagittarius; March 8 it will be 3° south of β Capricorni; and April 4 it will be 9° south of γ Aquarii, the brightest star in the Urn.

.MARS will be Evening Star during the entire year. It will appear largest January 10, being then at its opposition, or 180° from the Sun, and rising about sunset. It is then nearest the Earth, and its diameter about four times as large as when at its conjunction. On April 15, it will be 90° east of the Sun, and pass the meridian about sunset. On January 1, it will be south-east of Pollux, and about on a line with Castor and Pollux. It moves backwards or to the west now, and until February 18. On January 7, it will be 2½° south of Pollux; on January 14, 6° south of Castor; and on April 7, it will be back again due south of Pollux, but now 4½° south of it, and 18° north of Procyon. After June the planet will be rather inconspicuous.

JUPITER will be Evening Star until February 3, being then in conjunction with the Sun, and lost in its light. Thence Morning Star until May 27, when it reaches its western quadrature. During the rest of the year it will be Evening Star, and rather interesting. August 26, it will be largest and at the opposition, rising about sunset, and will appear three times as large as Mars did on January 10. Its positions in the sky are shown for the year in the engraving. On December 9 it will be 10° due south of the brightest star in the Urn.

SATURN will be Morning Star until February 12, rising after this before midnight, and being Evening Star until November 19, when it becomes Morning Star. It will be in Libra most of the year, north-west of Antares, and at the time of opposition, May 12, it will be brightest. See the drawing of its path.

MERCURY will be brightest, and at the most favorable stations for visibility, March 6, July 3, and October 28, being then in the west, and Evening Star soon after sunset; also April 25, August 24, and December 12, being then in the east as Morning Star just before sunrise.

NOTABLE DAYS AND PERIODS.

Dominical Letter, F; Epact, 25; Golden Number, 6; Solar Cycle, 28; Julian Period, 6,580; Jewish Lunar Cycle, 3; Dionysian Period, 196.

The 92d year of American Independence begins July 4; the 5,628th of the Jews begins September 30; the 1,284th of Mohammed begins May 5th, and ends April 23, 1868.

ANCIENT DATES.—Astronomers have been enabled to fix the dates of many events in ancient history, by means of the natural phenomena recorded in connection with them by historians. Thus a battle between the Medes and the Lydians is proved to have been fought May 28, B. C. 585; for there was a total eclipse of the sun during its progress, and unerring calculations prove that the only eclipse total in Asia Minor at that era was on the day above named. In a similar manner Halley ascertained the precise day of the landing of Julius Cæsar in Britain, August 26, B. C. 55, guided by the notices in Cæsar's Commentaries respecting the full moon and the tides. Some of the dates thus determined by modern science are of importance, as they help to fix the time of other memorable events.

THE TRACK OF SATURN,

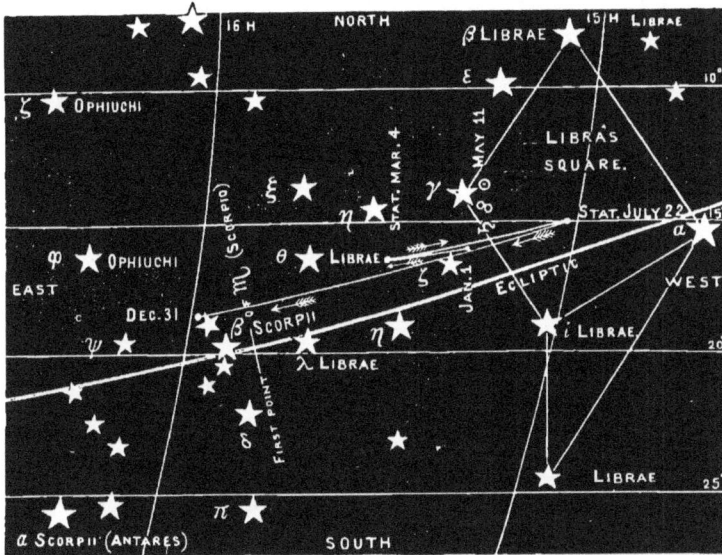

Showing its direct and retrograde motions. It retrogrades from March 4 to July 22.

THE PATH OF MARS, WHEN NEAR THE OPPOSITION,

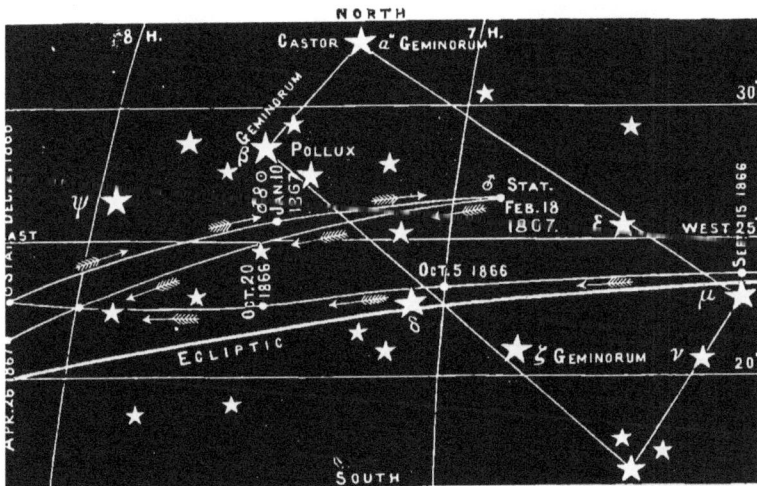

Showing his direct and retrograde motions. He retrogrades, or moves westward, from December 2, 1866, to February 18. 1867. He then moves eastward the rest of the year.

1*

PHASES OF VENUS.

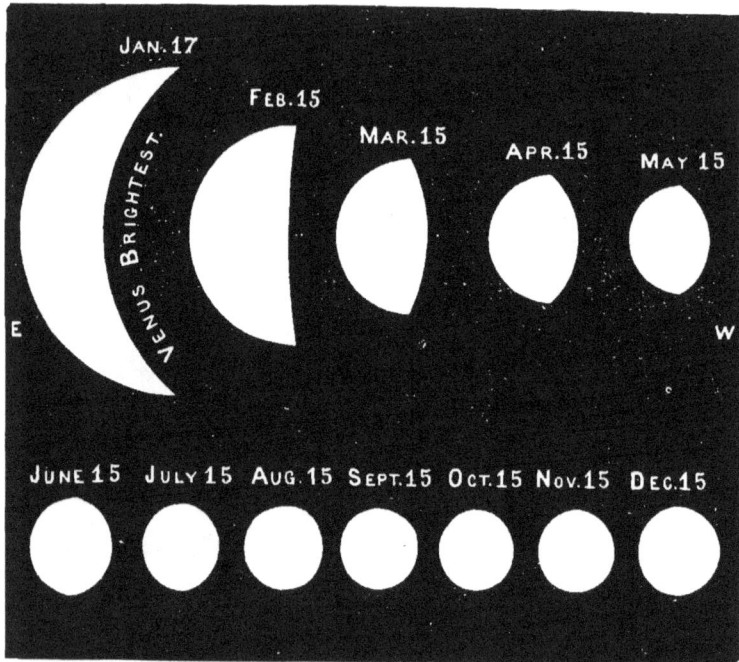

JAN. 17

VENUS BRIGHTEST.

FEB. 15

MAR. 15

APR. 15

MAY 15

E

W

JUNE 15   JULY 15   AUG. 15   SEPT. 15   OCT. 15   NOV. 15   DEC. 15

THE PATH OF JUPITER IN THE SKY,

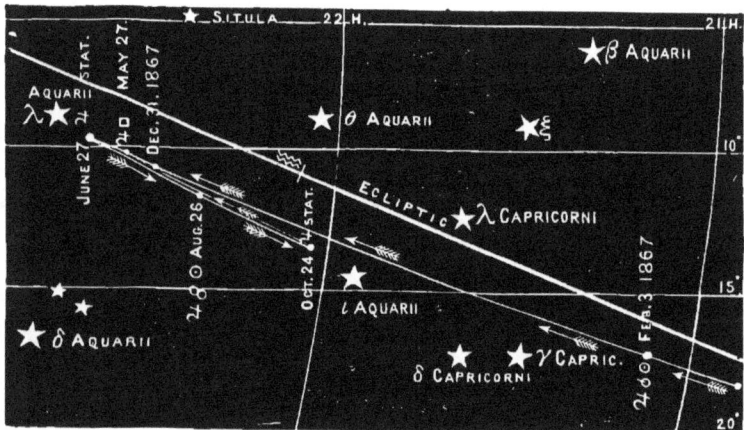

★ S. TULA   22 H.   21 H.

★β AQUARII

STAT.
MAY 27.

DEC. 7, 1867

AQUARII
λ ★ ♃

★ θ AQUARII

★ξ

JUNE 27

♃ □

♃ ☉ AUG. 26

STAT.

ECLIPTIC
★ λ CAPRICORNI

10°

OCT. 24

FEB. 3, 1867

★

ι AQUARII

15°

♃ ☉

★
★ δ AQUARII

★
δ CAPRICORNI

★ γ CAPRIC.
♃ δ ☉

20°

Showing his direct and retrograde motions.   He moves back, or towards the west, past the stars, from June 27 to October 24.   At other times he moves eastward.

1st MONTH.　　JANUARY, 1867.　　31 DAYS.

MOON'S PHASES.		BOSTON.	NEW YORK.	WASH'TON.	CHARLES'N.	Sun on Merid.		
	D.	H. M.	H. M.	H. M.	H. M.	D.	H. M. S.	
New Moon	5	7 46 ev.	7 34 ev.	7 22 ev.	7 10 ev.	1	12 3 50	
First Quarter	13	11 50 mo.	11 38 mo.	11 26 mo.	11 14 mo.	9	12 7 24	
Full Moon	20	2 52 mo.	2 40 mo.	2 28 mo.	2 16 mo.	17	12 10 23	
Third Quarter	27	10 3 mo.	9 51 mo.	9 39 mo.	9 27 mo.	25	12 12 36	

The lower portion of the page consists of dense daily calendar tables for Charleston (North Carolina, Tennessee, Georgia, Alabama, Mississippi, and Louisiana); Washington (Maryland, Virginia, Missouri, Kentucky, and California); New York City and Philadelphia (Connecticut, New Jersey, Pennsylvania, Ohio, Indiana, and Illinois); and Boston (New England, New York State, Michigan, Wisconsin, Iowa, and Oregon), together with columns for Sun's declination South, Day of Week, Day of Month, and Day of Year.

2d MONTH.	FEBRUARY, 1867.			28 DAYS.

MOON'S PHASES.	BOSTON.	NEW YORK.	WASH'TON.	CHARLES'N.	Sun on Merid. or noon mark.
	D.	H. M.	H. M.	H. M.	H. M.	D. H. M. S.
New Moon	4	1 32 ev.	1 20 ev.	1 8 ev.	0 56 ev.	1 12 13 52
First Quarter	11	8 56 ev.	8 44 ev.	8 32 ev.	8 20 ev.	9 12 14 29
Full Moon	18	2 57 ev.	2 45 ev.	2 33 ev.	2 21 ev.	17 12 14 16
Third Quarter	26	6 48 mo.	6 36 mo.	6 24 mo.	6 12 mo.	25 12 13 18

CALENDAR FOR CHARLES'N; NORTH Carolina, Tennessee, Geo., Alabama, Mississippi, and Louisiana.

SUN RISES.	SUN SETS.	MOON RISES.	H. W. CH'TON.
6 55	5 33	4 19	5 32
6 55	5 34	5 6	6 7
6 54	5 34	5 50	7 4
6 54	5 35	6 45	8 9
6 53	5 36	7 43	9 6
6 52	5 37	8 43	10 3½
6 52	5 38	9 42	11 17
6 51	5 39	10 43	morn.
6 50	5 40	11 43	0 7
6 49	5 41	morn.	1 15
6 48	5 42	0 45	2 23
6 47	5 43	1 48	3 32
6 47	5 44	2 50	4 35
6 45	5 45	3 49	5 31
6 45	5 46	4 44	6 31
6 44	5 47	5 35	7 19
6 42	5 48	rises.	8 6
6 41	5 48	6 57	8 47
6 40	5 49	7 55	9 29
6 39	5 50	8 54	10 11
6 37	5 51	9 51	10 52
6 36	5 53	10 46	11 36
6 34	5 54	11 40	morn. ev. 21
6 33	5 55	morn.	0 15
6 32	5 56	0 32	1 11
6 31	5 57	1 22	2 8
6 30	5 58	2 12	3

CALENDAR FOR WASHINGTON; Mary'd, Virg'a, Ken'y, Missouri, and California.

SUN RISES.	SUN SETS.	MOON RISES.
7 ...	5 21	4 31
7 ...	5 23	5 19
7 ...	5 24	sets.
7 ...	5 25	6 39
7 ...	5 26	7 40
7 ...	5 27	8 42
7 ...	5 29	9 44
7 5	5 30	10 47
6 59	5 31	11 50
6 58	5 33	morn.
6 57	5 34	0 55
6 55	5 35	2 0
6 54	5 36	3 ...
6 53	5 37	4 ...
6 52	5 38	4 56
6 51	5 40	5 45
6 49	5 41	rises.
6 48	5 42	6 54
6 47	5 44	7 57
6 46	5 45	8 56
6 44	5 46	9 55
6 42	5 47	10 53
6 40	5 48	11 49
6 39	5 50	morn.
6 37	5 51	0 43
6 36	5 52	1 34
6 34	5 53	2 24

CALENDAR FOR N. YORK CITY; PHILadelphia, Conn., NewJersey, Penn'la, Ohio, Indiana, and Illinois.

SUN RISES.	SUN SETS.	MOON RISES.	H. W. N.YORK.
7 11	5 18	4 36	6 18
7 10	5 19	5 23	7 6
7 9	5 20	sets.	7 48
7 8	5 21	6 36	8 28
7 7	5 22	7 39	9 11
7 6	5 23	8 42	9 52
7 5	5 25	9 45	10 40
7 4	5 26	10 49	11 14
7 2	5 28	11 53	morn.
7 1	5 30	morn.	0 2
7 0	5 31	0 58	0 54
6 58	5 32	2 0	1 53
6 57	5 33	3 ...	2 58
6 56	5 34	4 ...	3 6
6 55	5 36	4 59	4 5
6 53	5 37	5 48	5 17
6 52	5 39	rises.	6 21
6 51	5 40	6 53	7 16
6 49	5 41	7 56	8 ...
6 48	5 43	8 55	8 50
6 46	5 44	9 55	9 33
6 45	5 45	10 56	10 14
6 43	5 46	11 52	10 53
6 42	5 48	ev. 22	11 36
6 40	5 49	0 46	ev. 22
6 39	5 50	1 39	1 11
6 37	5 51	2 28	2 57
			3 53

CALENDAR FOR BOSTON; NEW ENGland, New York State, Michigan, Wisconsin, Iowa, and Oregon.

SUN RISES.	SUN SETS.	MOON RISES.	H. W. BOSTON.
7 14	5 14	4 40	9 32
7 13	5 15	5 27	10 20
7 12	5 16	sets.	11 ...
7 11	5 18	6 35	11 46
7 10	5 19	7 37	morn.
7 9	5 21	8 40	0 24
7 8	5 22	9 46	1 12
7 6	5 23	10 51	1 48
7 5	5 24	11 55	2 32
7 4	5 26	morn.	3 17
7 2	5 29	1 ...	4 7
7 1	5 30	2 3	5 12
6 59	5 32	3 4	6 23
6 57	5 33	4 5	7 33
6 56	5 35	5 ...	8 32
6 55	5 36	rises.	9 31
6 53	5 38	6 52	10 31
6 52	5 39	7 56	11 19
6 50	5 40	8 58	ev. 19
6 49	5 42	9 59	0 47
6 47	5 43	10 55	1 29
6 45	5 45	11 50	2 52
6 44	5 46	morn.	3 36
6 42	5 47	0 50	4 24
6 41	5 49	1 42	5 11
6 39	5 50	2 32	6 5
6 35	5 51		7 ...

Sun's decl. S.	Day of Week.	Day of Month.	Day of Year.
17 4 45	Fr	1	32
16 47 32	Sa	2	33
16 29 59	S	3	34
16 12 9	M	4	35
15 54 2	Tu	5	36
15 35 39	W	6	37
15 17 0	Th	7	38
14 58 5	Fr	8	39
14 38 55	Sa	9	40
14 19 33	S	10	41
13 59 57	M	11	42
13 40 8	Tu	12	43
13 20 5	W	13	44
12 59 50	Th	14	45
12 39 22	Fr	15	46
12 18 42	Sa	16	47
11 57 51	S	17	48
11 36 48	M	18	49
11 15 33	Tu	19	50
10 54 8	W	20	51
10 31 53	Th	21	52
10 10 36	Fr	22	53
9 48 24	Sa	23	54
9 26 11	S	24	55
9 3 9	M	25	56
8 41 1	Tu	26	57
8 19 32	W	27	58
7 56 24	Th	28	59

3d MONTH.   MARCH, 1867.   31 DAYS.

MOON'S PHASES.		BOSTON.	NEW YORK.	WASH'TON.	CHARLES'N.	Sun on Merid.
	D.	H. M.	H. M.	H. M.	H. M.	D. H. M. S.
New Moon	6	4 54 mo.	4 42 mo.	4 30 mo.	4 18 mo.	1 12 12 34
First Quarter	13	4 3 mo.	3 51 mo.	3 39 mo.	3 27 mo.	9 12 10 45
Full Moon	20	4 11 mo.	3 59 mo.	3 47 mo.	3 35 mo.	17 12 8 33
Third Quarter	28	3 2 mo.	2 50 mo.	2 38 mo.	2 26 mo.	25 12 6 7

The body of this page consists of dense monthly calendar tables giving Sun rises, Sun sets, Moon rises, and High Water times for the latitudes of:

- CALENDAR FOR CHARLESTON, NORTH Carolina, Tennessee, Geo., Alabama, Mississippi, and Louisiana.
- CALENDAR FOR WASHINGTON, Maryland, Virg'a, Kent'y, Missouri, and California.
- CALENDAR FOR N. YORK CITY; PHILadelphia, Conn., New Jersey, Penn'a, Ohio, Indiana, and Illinois.
- CALENDAR FOR BOSTON, NEW ENGland, New York State, Michigan, Wisconsin, Iowa, and Oregon.

with additional columns for Sun's decl. S., Day of Week, Day of Month, and Day of Year (60–90).

4th MONTH.	APRIL, 1867.	30 DAYS.

MOON'S PHASES.		BOSTON.	NEW YORK.	WASH'TON.	CHARLES'N.	Sun on Merid. or noon mark.			
	D.	H. M.	H. M.	H. M.	H. M.	D.	H.	M.	S.
New Moon	4	5 20 ev.	5 8 ev.	4 56 ev.	4 44 ev.	1	12	3	58
First Quarter	11	10 25 mo.	10 13 mo.	10 1 mo.	9 49 mo.	9	12	1	39
Full Moon	18	6 22 ev.	6 10 ev.	5 58 ev.	5 46 ev.	17	11	59	35
Third Quarter	26	9 17 ev.	9 5 ev.	8 53 ev	8 41 ev.	25	11	57	54

| 5th MONTH. | | MAY, 1867. | | | | 31 DAYS. | |

MOON'S PHASES.

MOON'S PHASES.	D.	BOSTON.	NEW YORK.	WASH'TON.	CHARLES'N.	Sun on Merid. or noon mark.		
		H. M.	H. M.	H. M.	H. M.	D.	M. M.	S.
New Moon	4	2 56 mo.	2 44 mo.	2 32 mo.	2 20 mo.	1	11	57	0
First Quarter	10	5 20 ev.	5 8 ev.	4 56 ev.	4 44 ev.	9	11	56	17
Full Moon	18	9 8 mo.	8 56 mo.	8 44 mo.	8 32 mo.	17	11	56	10
Third Quarter	26	0 38 ev.	0 26 ev.	0 14 ev.	0 2 ev.	25	11	56	39

CALENDAR FOR CHARLES'N; NORTH Carolina, Tennessee, Geo, Alabama, Missis- sippi, and Louisiana.

H. W. Ch'ton	Moon rises.	Sun sets.	Sun rises.
5 32	3 30	6 42	5 13.6
6 22	4 10	6 43	5 12.6
7 11	4 52	6 44	5 11.6
7 57	sets.	6 45	5 10.6
8 47	8 21	6 45	5 9.6
9 40	9 25	6 46	5 8.6
10 35	10 26	6 47	5 7.6
11 43	11 22	6 47	5 6.6
morn.	morn.	6 48	5 6.6
0 29	0 12	6 49	5 4.6
1 31	0 57	6 49	5 3.6
2 31	1 39	6 50	5 2.6
3 26	2 16	6 51	5 1.6
4 15	2 52	6 52	5 0.6
5 0	3 27	6 52	4 59.6
5 45	4 4	6 53	4 58.6
6 24	4 40	6 54	4 57.6
7 8	rises.	6 54	4 56.6
8 43	7 51	6 55	4 56.6
9 25	8 42	6 56	4 55.6
10 5	9 29	6 56	4 55.6
10 47	10 13.	6 57	4 54.7
11 32	10 34.	6 58	4 54.7
ev. 20	11 11.	6 59	4 53.7
0 11	morn.	7 0	4 53.7
1 7	0 12	7 0	4 52.7
2 4	0 49	7 1	4 52.7
3 5	1 25	7 2	4 52.7
4 5	2 3	7 2	4 51.7
5 56	2 43	7 2	4 51.7
	3 26	7 3	4 53.7

CALENDAR FOR WASHINGTON; Mary'd, Virg'a, Ken'y, Missouri, and California.

H. W. Wash.	Moon rises.	Sun sets.	Sun rises.
3 30	3 47	6 52	5 26
4 7	4 46	6 53	5 16
4 46		6 54	5 0
sets.		6 54	4 59
8 33	8 56	6 56	4 58
9 38	9 57	6 57	4 57
10 30	10 58	6 58	4 56
11 34	11 59	6 59	4 54
0 morn.	0 morn.	6 59	4 53
0 22	1 2	7 0	4 52
1 5	2 1	7 1	4 51
2 1	2 44	7 2	4 50
2 58	3 21	7 2	4 50
3 51	3 56	7 3	4 49
4 24	4 32	7 4	4 48
5 7	5 7	7 4	4 48
6 8	rises.	7 5	4 47
8 55	8 18	7 5	4 46
9 41	9 8	7 6	4 45
10 25	9 54	7 7	4 44
11 43	10 27	7 8	4 43
morn.	11 2	7 9	4 43
0 18	11 32	7 10	4 41
0 54	morn.	7 11	4 40
1 27	0 7	7 12	4 40
2 39	0 42	7 13	4 39
3 19	1 24	7 13	4 38
	2 3	7 15	4 38
	2 39	7 16	4 38
	3 19	7 17	4 37
		7 18	4 37

CALENDAR FOR N. YORK CITY; Phil- adelphia, Conn., New Jersey, Penn'a, Ohio, Indiana, and Illinois.

H. W. N'York	Moon rises.	Sun sets.	Sun rises.
6 18	3 30	6 56	4 59
7 8	4 6	6 57	4 58
7 53	4 45	6 58	4 58
8 42	sets.	6 59	4 56
9 33	8 36	0	4 54.7
10 24	9 43	7	4 53.7
11 morn.	10 44	7	4 52.7
0 16	11 37	7	4 51.7
0 25	morn.	7	4 51.7
1 17	0 1	7	4 49.7
2 14	0 45	7	4 48.7
3 17	1 29	7	4 47.7
4 11	2 19	7	4 46.7
5 46	2 51	7	4 45.7
6 29	3 23	7	4 44.7
7 7	3 55	7	4 43.7
8 48	4 29	7	4 41.7
9 29	rises.	7	4 40.7
10 11	8 59	7	4 39.7
10 47	9 46	7	4 38.7
11 11	10 30	7	4 37.7
ev. 18	10 44	7	4 36.7
1 57	morn.	7	4 35.7
2 53	0 21	7	4 34.7
3 49	0 55	7	4 34.7
4 46	1 27	7	4 33.7
5 45	2 37	7	4 33.7
6 42	3 17	7	4 32.7
		7	4 31.7

CALENDAR FOR BOSTON; NEW ENG- land, New York State, Michigan, Wisconsin, Iowa, and Oregon.

H. W. Boston	Moon rises.	Sun sets.	Sun rises.
9 32	3 30	0	4 56.7
10 22	4 5	1	4 54.7
11 11	4 43	2	4 53.7
11 57	sets.	3	4 52.7
morn.	8 40	4	4 51.7
0 47	9 47	5	4 49.7
1 40	10 48	6	4 48.7
2 35	11 41	7	4 47.7
3 43	morn.	8	4 46.7
4 29	0 28	9	4 45.7
5 31	1 10	10	4 43.7
6 31	1 47	12	4 42.7
7 32	2 20	13	4 41.7
8 26	2 51	14	4 40.7
9 15	3 22	15	4 39.7
10 0	3 53	16	4 37.7
10 45	4 27	17	4 36.7
11 24	rises.	18	4 35.7
ev.	9 11	19	4 34.7
0 43	9 50	20	4 33.7
1 25	10 33	21	4 32.7
2 4	11 48	22	4 31.7
2 47	morn.	23	4 31.7
3 32	0 23	24	4 30.7
4 20	0 56	25	4 29.7
5 7	1 28	26	4 29.7
6 4	2 1	27	4 28.7
7 4	2 36	28	4 28.7
8 9	3 13	29	4 27.7
9 56	3 15	29	4 26.7

Main Calendar

Day of Year.	Day of Month.	Day of Week.	Sun's decl. N.	
121	1	W	15 4.59	
122	2	Th	15 23.3	
123	3	Fr	15 40.47	
124	4	Sa	15 58.18	
125	5	18	16 15.33	
126	6	M	16 32.31	
127	7	Tu	16 49.31	
128	8	W	17 5.39	
129	9	Th	17 21.47	
130	10	Fr	17 37.11	
131	11	Sa	17 53.26	
132	12	19	18 8.1	
133	13	M	18 23.20	
134	14	Tu	18 38.23	
135	15	W	18 52.25	
136	16	Th	19 6.5	
137	17	Fr	19 20.26	
138	18	Sa	19 33.33	
139	19	20	19 46.20	
140	20	M	19 59.5	
141	21	Tu	20 11.23	
142	22	W	20 23.9	
143	23	Th	20 35.0	
144	24	Fr	20 46.36	
145	25	Sa	20 57.55	
146	26	21	21 7.9	
147	27	M	21 18.0	
148	28	Tu	21 28.36	
149	29	W	21 37.55	
150	30	Th	21 46.36	
151	31	Fr	21 55.20	

| 6th MONTH. | JUNE, 1867. | | | 30 DAYS. |

MOON'S PHASES.		BOSTON.	NEW YORK.	WASH'TON.	CHARLES'N.	Sun on Merid. or noon mark.
	D.	H. M.	H. M.	H. M.	H. M.	D. H. M. S.
New Moon	2	10 28 mo.	10 16 mo.	10 4 mo.	9 52 mo.	1 11 57 31
First Quarter	9	1 53 mo.	1 41 mo.	1 29 mo.	1 17 mo.	9 11 58 54
Full Moon	16	0 10 mo.	11 58 ev.	11 46 ev.	11 34 ev.	17 12 0 32
Third Quarter	25	0 45 mo.	0 33 mo.	0 21 mo.	0 9 mo.	25 12 2 15

The detailed daily calendar columns (Calendars for Charleston; Washington; New York City; and Boston, with Sun rises, Sun sets, Moon sets, High Water, Sun's declination, Day of Week, Day of Month, Day of Year) are rendered in fine rotated print and not fully transcribable.

7th MONTH.   JULY, 1867.   31 DAYS.

MOON'S PHASES.		BOSTON.	NEW YORK.	WASH'TON.	CHARLES'N.	Sun on Merid.		
	D.	H. M.	H. M.	H. M.	H. M.	D.	H.	M. S.
New Moon	1	5 4 ev.	4 52 ev.	4 40 ev	4 28 ev.	1	12	3 29
First Quarter	8	0 47 ev.	0 35 ev.	0 23 ev.	0 11 ev.	9	12	4 53
Full Moon	16	3 12 ev.	3 0 ev.	2 48 ev.	2 36 ev	17	12	5 49
Third Quarter	24	9 52 me.	9 40 mo.	9 28 mo.	9 16 mo.	25	12	6 13
New Moon	30	11 59 ev.	11 47 ev.	11 35 ev.	11 23 ev.			

The lower portion of the page consists of dense calendar tables for Charleston (North Carolina, Tennessee, Georgia, Alabama, Mississippi, and Louisiana); Washington (Maryland, Virginia, Kentucky, Missouri, and California); New York City & Philadelphia (Connecticut, New Jersey, Pennsylvania, Ohio, Indiana, and Illinois); and Boston (New England states, New York State, Michigan, Wisconsin, Iowa, and Oregon), together with columns for Sun's declination N., Day of Week, Day of Month, and Day of Year.

8th MONTH.	AUGUST, 1867.	31 DAYS.

MOON'S PHASES.	BOSTON.	NEW YORK.	WASH'TON.	CHARLES'N	Sun on Merid. or noon mark.
	D. H. M.	H. M.	H. M.	H. M.	D. H. M. S.
First Quarter 7	2 24 mo.	2 12 mo.	2 0 mo.	1 48 mo.	1 12 6 4
Full Moon ------ 15	5 53 mo.	5 41 mo.	5 29 mo.	5 17 mo.	9 12 5 17
Third Quarter ·· 22	4 38 ev.	4 26 ev.	4 14 ev.	4 2 ev.	17 12 3 53
New Moon ······ 29	8 21 mo.	8 9 mo.	7 57 mo.	7 45 mo.	25 12 1 57

CALENDAR FOR CHARLES'N, NORTH Carolina, Tennessee, Geo., Alabama, Mississippi, and Louisiana.

CALENDAR FOR WASHINGTON, Mary'd, Virg'a, Ken'y, Missouri, and California.

CALENDAR FOR N. YORK CITY, PHILADELPHIA, Conn., New Jersey, Penn'a, Ohio, Indiana, and Illinois.

CALENDAR FOR BOSTON, NEW ENGLAND, New York State, Michigan, Wisconsin, Iowa, and Oregon.

9th MONTH. SEPTEMBER, 1867. 30 DAYS.

MOON'S PHASES.	D.	BOSTON. H. M.	NEW YORK. H. M.	WASH'TON. H. M.	CHARLES'N. H. M	Sun on Merid. or noon mark. D. H. M. S.
First Quarter	5	6 47 ev.	6 35 ev.	6 23 ev.	6 11 ev.	1 11 59 54
Full Moon	13	7 49 ev.	7 37 ev.	7 25 ev.	7 13 ev.	9 11 57 16
Third Quarter	20	10 21 ev.	10 9 ev.	9 57 ev.	9 45 ev.	17 11 54 28
New Moon	27	6 58 ev.	6 46 ev.	6 34 ev.	6 22 ev.	25 11 51 41

The main body of this page is a multi-region calendar table giving, for each of the 30 days of September 1867, the Sun rises, Sun sets, Moon sets, and High Water times for four regions:

- CALENDAR FOR CHARLES'N, NORTH Carolina, Tennessee, Geo., Alabama, Mississippi, and Louisiana.
- CALENDAR FOR WASHINGTON, Mary'd, Virg'a, Ken'y, Missouri, and California.
- CALENDAR FOR N. YORK CITY, PHILadelphia, Conn., New Jersey, Penn'a, Ohio, Indiana, and Illinois.
- CALENDAR FOR BOSTON, NEW ENGland, New York State, Michigan, Wisconsin, Iowa, and Oregon.

Additional columns give the Sun's decl. N., Day of Week, Day of Month, and Day of Year.

10th MONTH. OCTOBER, 1867. 31 DAYS.

MOON'S PHASES.	D.	BOSTON. H. M.	NEW YORK. H. M.	WASH'TON. H. M.	CHARLES'N. H. M.	Sun on Merid. D.	H. M. S.
First Quarter	5	1 33 ev.	1 21 ev.	1 9 ev.	0 57 ev.	1	11 49 42
Full Moon	13	8 40 mo.	8 28 mo.	8 16 mo.	8 4 mo.	9	11 47 20
Third Quarter	20	4 33 mo.	4 21 mo.	4 9 mo.	3 57 mo.	17	11 45 26
New Moon	27	8 19 mo.	8 7 mo.	7 55 mo.	7 43 mo.	25	11 44 11

(The remainder of the page consists of dense regional calendar tables printed sideways for Charleston (North Carolina, Tennessee, Georgia, Alabama, Mississippi, and Louisiana); Washington (Maryland, Virginia, Kentucky, Missouri, and California); New York City, Philadelphia, etc. (Connecticut, New Jersey, Pennsylvania, Ohio, Indiana, and Illinois); and Boston (New England, New York State, Michigan, Wisconsin, Iowa, and Oregon), together with columns for Sun's declination, Day of Week, Day of Month, and Day of Year.)

11th MONTH.   NOVEMBER, 1867.   30 DAYS.

MOON'S PHASES.	D.	BOSTON. H. M.	NEW YORK. H. M.	WASH'TON. H. M.	CHARLES'N. H. M.	Sun on Merid. or noon mark. D. H. M. S.
First Quarter	4	9 43 mo.	9 31 mo.	9 19 mo.	9 7 mo.	1 11 43 42
Full Moon	11	8 26 ev.	8 14 ev.	8 2 ev.	7 50 ev.	9 11 43 57
Third Quarter	18	0 22 ev.	0 10 ev.	11 58 mo.	11 46 mo.	17 11 45 6
New Moon	26	0 27 mo.	0 15 mo.	0 3 mo.	11 51 ev.	25 11 47 8

12th MONTH.	DECEMBER, 1867.	31 DAYS.

MOON'S PHASES.		BOSTON.	NEW YORK.	WASH'TON.	CHARLES'N.	Sun on Merid.
	D.	H. M.	H. M.	H. M.	H. M.	D.	H. M. S.
First Quarter	4	5 36 mo.	5 24 mo.	5 12 mo.	5 0 mo.	1	11 49 12
Full Moon	11	7 26 mo.	7 14 mo.	7 2 mo.	6 50 mo.	9	11 52 31
Third Quarter	17	10 50 ev.	10 38 ev.	10 26 ev.	10 14 ev.	17	11 56 18
New Moon	25	6 55 ev.	6 43 ev.	6 31 ev.	6 19 ev.	25	12 0 17

EVERY hour that flits so slowly
  Has its task to do or bear ;
Luminous the crown, and holy,
  If thou set each gem with care.

Hours are golden links, God's token,
  Reaching heaven ; but one by one
Use them, lest the chain be broken
  Ere thy pilgrimage be done.

George, or Answered Prayer.

George was a child of believing parents. He descended from a
long line of believing ancestry, and thus was heir of the promises and
prayers which belong to the "children's children." Every thing that
parental love and assiduity could do for him, was done ; and George
grew up as fine a lad as could be found. He was correct in his principles, correct in his speech, correct in all his habits. The mistake of
a dime in his accounts, when in business, would have put him to a
month's labor rather than not to have discovered it. Full of energy,
he was more than ordinarily successful in getting a situation which
promised well for this life.

Strange it is that this very sense of correctness often antagonizes
the doctrines of the cross. It shrinks from them as something too
hard and humbling. He could not understand, he said, the faith of
his fathers ; it was beyond his calculations—fore-knowledge and free-
will, trinity in unity, the cross and the crown ; and so he drifted to
where all these are set aside, an easier faith.

"Well, my son," said his father, after many a faithful conversation,
"if you are determined to go, I can do no more. We will talk no
more over it ; but your mother and I shall never cease to pray for you."
George remained dutiful and affectionate ; the parents loving with a
depth of yearning tenderness which none but parents know.

George was taken ill. He rallied, but slowly. He left the desk,

3

and gave himself up to air and exercise. He was better, but not well. There was a certain something, no one could tell exactly what, which indicated failing. The doctors advised a journey—time, rest. A leisurely excitement would bring him up, they said; there was nothing to fear, every thing to hope.

His letters were buoyant with youthful spirits, and all contained, " better, mother ; better, father ;" until, after a longer interval, came a telegram, short, sharp, decisive : " George is ill ; come," etc., mentioning a far-off western village. The parents set off on their long and unlooked-for journey. Amid bewildering snow-storms they pushed rapidly on ; no pause, night or day, until they reached the dear object of their quest.

But such a greeting ! " Dear mother," said the dying young man, " I have found your Saviour." George lived many days, the parents hoping against hope, and rejoicing in the joy of the lost one found. Just how and where the Good Shepherd found his lamb, was deferred until he had more strength to tell the blessed story ; but the strength never came, and it remains to be told in the glory that shall be revealed. There were a few days of blessed communion, parents and child, with Father, Son, and Holy Ghost, all barriers broken down, and each with each tasting the sweets of redeeming love. Their wrestling prayer was answered ; but how little did they expect to find its answer in a far-off village of the West.   H. C. K.

A WORLDLY spirit says, " Time is short ; take your fill : live while you can." A narrow religious spirit says, "All pleasure here is a snare, and dangerous ; keep out of it altogether." Christianity says, in opposition to the one, " Use the world ;" in opposition to the other, " Do not abuse it. All things are yours. Take them and use them ; but never let them interfere with the higher life which you are called to lead. A man's life consisteth not in the abundance of the things that he possesses."

It is therefore a distinct duty to use life while we are here. We are citizens of the world ; we may not shrink from it. We must share its dangers, duties, joys, and sorrows. Time is short; therefore opportunities are so much the more valuable. There is an infinite value stamped upon them. *Use* the world ; but then it is a duty equally distinct to live *above* the world. An unworldly spirit will hold all things as not its own, in the perpetual conviction that they will not last. It is not to put life and God's lovely world aside with self-torturing hand. It is to have the world, and not let the world have you ; to be its master, and not its slave ; to have Christ hidden in the heart, calming all, and making all else seem by comparison poor and small.

Snow, snow, snow! What a simple, careless, thoughtless, aimless motion has a snow-flake. It rests on a leaf and lights on the ground and touches the fences with such a quiet, dainty softness. If any one should ask what is the most harmless and innocent thing on earth, we might say, A snow-flake. And yet what a power is in it. When it fills the air, neither hunter or pilot, guide or watchman is any better than a blind man. When it pours over the hills and lurks down in the valleys, it will in a single night entrench itself, and bid defiance to human strength. All the kings of the earth could not enforce an edict upon mankind, "Let labor cease." But this white-flowered light-infantry clears out the field, drives men home, and puts a continent under ban. It is a despiser of old landmarks, unites all properties, covers up fences, hides paths and roads, doing in one day what the engineers and laborers of the whole earth could not do in years.

In a few weeks another silent force will come, and the victorious army of snow-flakes will be vanquished. A rain-drop is stronger than a snow-flake. One by one they will give up and descend into the earth, and dwell among the roots; and the bud will open its eye, the leaf shall lift up its head, the grass shall wave its spear, and the forests hang out their banners. How significant these slow, silent, resistless powers of God's truth in the world. "For as the rain cometh down, and the snow from heaven, and returneth not thither, but watereth the earth, and maketh it bring forth and bud, that it may give seed to the sower and bread to the eater; so shall my word be that goeth forth out of my mouth : it shall not return unto me void, but it shall accomplish that which I please, and it shall prosper in the thing whereto I sent it."

Not more Excitement, but more Piety.

Preaching that stirs us up to a sense of the peril of men under the law, and urges our responsibility in relation to it, possesses great power for a time ; but these feelings quickly wear out. It is impossible for even the best of people to live long under the influence of an excited conscience. They cannot bear it a great while. A reaction is sure to come. What we need is, to be brought into a more fervent love of God, more overflowing joy in the Holy Ghost, more of that faith which feeds and rests on Christ ; then the church will have food, not for forty days, but for forty years. We need an average level of feeling and action many times higher than that at present, where the feelings grow out of a higher class of Christian experience, which does not wear out. These promote health, and never leave the body and mind to that languor which necessarily succeeds excitement. They keep up the spiritual tone, and make Christian effort hearty and constant—a "needs be" of the "new man."

THERE is sorrow in the happy household at Bethany. Lazarus is sick, and Jesus is away beyond Jordan. The sisters hasten to send a messenger with the simple tidings, "Lord, behold, he whom thou lovest is sick." How beautiful is their confidence in him. They do not urge him to come; they only tell their need, sure that this will be enough. He does not leave and forsake them whom he loves. "This sickness is not unto death," was his answer; and yet, ere the messenger returned, Lazarus was dead. Could it be their divine Friend had deceived them, or had been deceived himself? Why had he not made the issue certain by himself coming; or if aught had hindered, by speaking that word which he had spoken for others, and they had been saved? But was it not like many a divine promise, which seems to us for the moment utterly to fail, because we know not the resources of divine love ?

Two days the Lord abode in Peræa. On the third day he set out for Bethany. Lazarus had been buried four days. Tarrying outside the town, Martha heard of his coming, and went to meet him, exclaiming, "Lord, if thou hadst been here, my brother had not died." Mary came, and falling on her knees, cried, "Lord, if thou hadst been here, my brother had not died ;" for it is the bitterest drop in their cup of anguish, that all this might have been otherwise. And how often, during that four days of sorrow, must this thought have been in their hearts and this word upon their lips.

"Thy brother shall rise again."

"I know that he shall rise again in the resurrection of the last day," said Martha.

"*I* am the resurrection and the life : he that believeth in me, though he were dead, yet shall he live : and whosoever liveth and believeth in me, shall never die." Wonderful and glorious words! taking no account of temporal death, but lifting the believer above death, and making him a present partaker of everlasting life. In me is victory over the grave ; in me is life eternal : by faith in me, *that* becomes yours which makes death not to be death, but only the transition to a higher life.

At the sight of so much grief around him, the sisters and friends weeping, Jesus himself was borne away with this great tide of sorrow, and went with the mourners to the grave. It was a cave. Such were commonly the family vaults of the Jews. Sometimes the entrance of these was on a level, sometimes there was a descent to them by steps. This was probably the case at Lazarus' grave, from the stone being said to lie *on* the tomb.

"Lazarus, come forth," is the quickening word ; at which life returns to the dead. "And he that was bound hand and foot with grave-clothes came forth." "Loose him, and let him go ;" and here the narrative ends, leaving us to imagine their joy who received their dead from the grave—a joy which, among the mourners of all time, was well-nigh theirs alone. K.

Heard From.

A clergyman residing in the country was unexpectedly called upon to preach on a Thanksgiving morning in a city church. He was a humble, self-distrustful man of God, and felt himself unfit to minister to so refined and intelligent an audience. What could *he* say to interest or profit them ? But it was plainly his Master's will, and he cast himself on his Master's promises for help. Thus feeling, he preached; and long did he look back upon that morning's labor with mortification and abasement.

Years went by. One day as he was cutting cornstalks in his field, a carriage came along. It stopped by the stone wall, and a gentleman called out, "Are you the Rev. Mr. —— ?"

"That is my name, sir."

"I am thankful to see you. I am glad to have the opportunity of thanking you for that Thanksgiving sermon which you preached at —— more than twenty years ago. It was just what I needed. It met my case. I never forgot it, and always hoped I should some time meet you to express my thanks to you for it."

Ah, little did this good man ever expect to hear thus from his sermon. So our works do follow us; and sometimes, long years after, they overtake us on our pilgrimage with blessing and encouragement.

K.

Soap and Water.

The neatness, order, and cleanliness of the poorer classes in Paris is as remarkable as it is refreshing. In the meanest eating-house the most delicate stomach would not be offended, nor the nicest garment soiled. The woman who serves you wears a clean dress, a fresh cap, and a tidy apron. You will have a napkin that reminds you of a sheet,

and in nine cases out of ten flowers will be set before you.   Ten children may be in the next room; but instead of animated dirt heaps,
such as one sees in most cities, these children could be kissed with
impunity.   The boot-black, from the nature of his occupation, appears
to be on less familiar terms with soap and water than any other of the
human family, and in England and America holds his rag and dirt as
prerogatives: but the Paris boot-black is always a man; he is always
clad in a uniform, generally of blue plush, and any lady might shake
hands with him without gloves and without fear.   The workmen also
have a uniform, or rather, they all dress alike, with white pants and
blue blouses.   There must be some law against rags, for the very beg-
gars wear the same white pants and blue frocks, cheap and coarse, but
decent-looking until utterly worn out.   The old women who sell gim-
cracks at street corners, and even the fat fishmongers in their greasy
stalls, look fresh and blooming as possible in their starched white caps
and clean calicoes.

The minor morals of soap and suds are surely not without their
value, and that labor and poverty are not necessarily inseparable from
dirt, is worth a voyage across the Atlantic to learn.   Can't the cheap
commodity, *cleanliness*, be somehow imported into this country, and
peddled pretty extensively ?

Education, to be Useful,

Must, as far as possible, be made simple, limited, practicable, accepta-
ble to the learner, adapted to his character and wants, and brought
home to his particular case by *subdivision* and *selection*.   The first step
should be for the interested to study, and as far as possible to ascertain
the peculiar bent and capacity of a boy's mind.   This being done, he
should be put upon a course of intellectual and physical training corresponding, as far as possible, to that for which nature seems to have
designed him; but in all cases a preparatory elementary education,
such as is furnished by our common schools, must be made a prerequi-
site even to qualify him to inquire; and the more thorough this preparatory training is made, the better it is for the student.

"RESOLVE to be a rich man.   Whatever else you get, be sure to get
wealth," said a father to his son; "that will give you influence in the
world : and remember, where there's a will, there's a way."

"But, father," said the lad seriously, "'how hardly shall they that
have riches enter into the kingdom of heaven.'   Does not the good
book say it is 'easier for a camel to go through the eye of a needle
than for a rich man to enter the kingdom of heaven ?'"

"When He shall Appear, We shall be like Him."

Oh mean may seem this house of clay,
    Yet 't was the Lord's abode ;
Our feet may mourn this thorny way,
    Yet here Immanuel trod.

This fleshly robe the Lord did wear,
    This watch the Lord did keep ;
These burdens sore the Lord did bear,
    These tears the Lord did weep.

Our very frailty brings us near
    Unto the Lord of heaven ;
To every grief, to every tear,
    Such glory strange is given.

But not this earthly robe alone
    Shall link us, Lord, to thee ;
Not always in the tear and groan
    Shall thy dear kindred be.

We shall be reckoned for thine own,
    Because thy heaven we share ;
Because we sing around thy throne,
    And thy bright raiment wear.

Christ's Dwelling-places.

The Lord Jesus *is* everywhere, but he is not said to *dwell* everywhere. Dwelling, with regard to him, implies preference, and abiding with him, delight. First then, he dwells in heaven; and this marks the place ; yea, this makes it. "Where I am, there shall my servants be." Secondly, he dwells in his church. "This," he says, "is my rest for ever ; here will I dwell." Thirdly, he dwells in the sanctuary. "In all *places* where I record my name, I will come unto thee, and I will bless thee." " *Where* two or three are gathered together in my name, there am *I* in the midst of them." And there his people have found him, and exclaimed, "Surely God is in this place." Fourthly, he dwells in the heart. "My son," he says, "give me thy heart ;" and from every believer he obtains what he demands. Christ dwells "in his heart by faith."

As in elder life we are filled with a strange and tender yearning for the spot where our childhood was passed, so do not the redeemed ones in heaven feel drawn with tenderness and love towards this earth, where the soul spent its childhood and took its first steps in the divine life ?
        *

Rest on Established Truths.

"Is it right and wise to read on both sides of religious questions ?"
I could not reply, No ; for that is the very advice given by the
Romish church, which we so much blame. But remember, the questions of religious truth are interminable, and a lifetime would scarcely
suffice to even pass the outworks of them all. Next, very few minds
are in possession of the means or of the severe mental training which
qualifies to set out as an original discoverer of the truth ; so that, if we
cannot begin with a large number of truths, which must be considered
as first principles and settled, life must be one perpetual state of
uncertainty.

On the other hand, to *refuse* to examine when doubts arise, is spiritual suicide ; and I do not see how, on this principle, any progress in
truth could ever have been made.

One consolation, however, at once suggests itself. The condition
of arriving at truth is not severe habits of investigation, but innocence
of life and nobleness of heart. Truth is felt, not reasoned out ; and if
there be any truths which are only appreciable by the acute understanding, we may be sure at once that they do not constitute the soul's
life, nor error in these the soul's death : for instance, the metaphysics
of God's being, the "plan of salvation," the exact distinction between
the divine and human in God's person. On all these questions you
may read until the brain is dizzy and the heart's action is stopped, so
that of course the mind is bewildered ; but on subjects of right and
wrong, divine and diabolic, noble and base, I believe sophistry cannot
puzzle so long as the heart and life are right.

I should say therefore,

1. Remember how much is certain. Is there any doubt about the
Sermon on the Mount ? whether, for instance, the Beatitudes are true
to fact—whether the pure in heart shall see God ? any doubt whether
to have the mind of Christ be salvation and rest ? Well, if the life-
truths are certain, you may be content to leave much, if God will, to
unfold itself slowly ; you can quietly wait for eternity to settle it.

2. The only thing that can be said is broadly this : I would not
read controversially. In this bewildered age, an age in which, like
Diana's worshippers, all are crying out loudly, the greater part not
knowing why, or what the questions really are, it seems to me that the
more we confine ourselves to simple duties the better. Be assured
that there is little to be known here, much to be borne, something to
be done.

Try rather to live upon the truths you have for certain, and let
them become firmer and firmer. How can you expect to fathom ques-

tions which the wisest of the age have been fathoming in vain ? This conviction once settled, I think we shall become content to wait—a great lesson—and let God teach us by degrees, instead of fancying we can find it all out by effort. We are anxious to know *all about* God, and meanwhile we never think of knowing *God*. God, instead of theology, is what we need to believe in.

"MY son is so fond of reading," said a mother, "he reads every thing and everywhere ;" and she was not the first mother who seemed to feel a flush of pride at this sign of intellectual precocity in her child.

Reading is no doubt the door of information and enlightenment, and taste for reading a source of pleasure and delightful employment for leisure hours that might be worse used : but let it never be forgotten, that it is a taste which needs much training ; first, in regard to the selection of books, and then as to the amount read.

Books, to be of real profit, either to strengthen or inform, must be judiciously *selected.* The swarm of books which yearly issue from the press make this imperative ; for, besides the positively bad books—books too which distil a *slow* poison, trashy and frivolous books—there are others which are unwholesome, because they contain so little nutriment, not enough to grow by.   They let down rather than lift up the mental powers. They form easy reading, to be sure, only *too easy.* A book is all the better for being above the average thought, in order to raise up and help forward. That is one object of reading. It is a great advantage for parents to read to and with their children, for they can interest and interpret books to them far above their ordinary understanding ; and one valuable book gone over in this way is worth a dozen read by a child himself.

Regard also the *amount* read. I tremble for a child "always reading ;" for to be always a passive recipient induces mental sloth, confusion, and repression.   Overfeeding is as bad for the mind as for the body.   Indeed I have known bright boys killed by intellectual gluttony—killed, I mean, for the real business of life.   Instead of becoming strong, wise, influential men, as might have been expected, they grew up do-nothings, bitterly disappointing their friends. Real work was a task.   Purpose and will seemed wanting. The fibre of the mind never toughening, as it cannot do except through exertion and use, could do little more than support their load of book knowledge, without ever attempting to turn it to any useful or profitable account.   K.

———————— • • ————————

To blame is easy enough ; with some, it is all of a piece with the hardness of their temperaments ; but to do this delicately, how shall we learn that ? I answer, *Love;* and then say what you will. Men will bear any thing if love be there.

———————— • • ————————

Putting Off.

It was my lot, said a shipmaster, to fall in with that ill-fated steamer the Central America.   Night was closing in, the sea rolling high, but I hailed the crippled steamer, and asked if they needed help.

"I am in a sinking condition," said Capt. Hernden.

"Had you not better send your passengers on board directly ?" I asked.

"Will you not lay by me till morning ?" asked the captain.

"I will try," I said; "but had you not better send your passengers on board *now?*"

"Lay by me till morning," was the answer.

I tried to ; but in one hour and a half after, the steamer and its living freight went down, and almost every one found a grave in the great deep.   But for this putting off, *all* might have been saved.

Another wreck and another warning on the shifting and bottomless sands of *Delay*.   As there are times and seasons in life when safety or success all depend upon a prompt recognition of "now or never ;" so in the soul's history, *now* is the accepted time, *now* is the day of salvation, when Christ is distinctly offered to us for our acceptance or rejection.   Every thing is imperilled by delay.   There is not a moment to spare.   Adverse currents and bewildering judgments may bear us away, and the opportunity be for ever lost of laying hold on the great anchor of hope for a lost and dying world.

SOMEBODY says, Let every farmer who has boys provide them a *workshop*.   We say, Let every *father* have a workshop, or work-room, or work-bench, where the boys may gratify their longing for tools, and incarnate their restless activity in "something to do."   It should be made pleasant, attractive, and comfortable.   If room enough, there can be a work-bench and vice, a shaving horse, and perhaps a small foot-lathe, two or three planes, augurs of different sizes, a few chisels, drawing-knife, saw, and hammer.   For those who cannot afford the whole, a part would answer ; and to those who can, other tools might be added, the cost of the tools being but a trifle compared with the advantages gained, one of which is a real progress in *practical education*. It has been said the best inheritance a man can leave his children is not money to maintain them, but the *ability to help and take care of themselves*.

A young man who can at any time mend sofa, chair, rocker, sled, harness, or tin ware, set the clock, repair an umbrella, whitewash a wall, paper a room, and do a hundred other small jobs, will get through the world far more comfortably and thriftily than one who is constantly obliged to send for a mechanic. Besides all this, and greater still, is the moral influence of tools in furnishing boys something cheerful to do in stormy weather or leisure hours, and thus weakening any temptation to attend those places of diversion which so often lay the foundation of life-long harm to character.

Forty-five.

By the time a man has reached forty-five or thereabouts, he lies as comfortably in his habits as the silkworm in its cocoon. He is contented with his old friends. He loves the fields which he sees every day, and would not exchange them for Niagara or the Alps. There is a certain even-handed justice in Time ; and for what he takes away, he gives us something in return. He robs us of elasticity, and in its place brings tranquillity and repose—the mild autumnal weather of the soul. He takes away hope, but he gives us memory. One has seen the good and the evil that are in the world, its ups and its downs, and has learned to be uncensorious and humane ; for in middle age, provided the man has been a good one, along with this mental tranquillity there comes a corresponding sweetness of the moral atmosphere. He has a hearty "amen" for every good wish, and in the worst cases leans to a verdict of Not proven. He is chary of imputing a sweeping and cruel blame, and has a certain grave humor which has pity lying at the bottom.

On the whole, I take it that middle age is a happier period than youth. In the entire circle of the year there are no days so delightful as those of a fine October, when the trees are bare to the mild heavens, and the red leaves bestrew the road, and you can feel the breath of winter moving—no days so calm, so tenderly solemn, and with such a reverent meekness in the air. There is an "unrest which men miscall delight," and of that unrest youth is for the most part composed. From that, middle age is free. The setting suns of youth are crimson and gold ; the setting suns of middle age

> "Do take a sober coloring from an eye
> That hath kept watch o'er man's mortality."

By a law of the state of Maine, any person who shall, to the acceptance of the selectmen, place a trough by the roadside, into which
a stream of water shall be kept constantly running, is entitled to an
annual deduction of three dollars from his taxes ; and who will not say
that it is wise and enlightened legislation ? I am sure the state fathers
had an eye not only to comfort, but to beauty and picturesqueness. It
is a statute too well becoming a state in the front ranks of temperance,
which, if severe and scrutinizing in its prohibitions against liquor, is
ever ready to furnish a cup of cold water to man and beast. Drinking
fountains opened at convenient places in our towns, cities, railway sta-

tions, and wherever there is sufficient travel to warrant it, would do more to undermine the profits of dram-shops and beer saloons than almost any thing else that can be done. In a thousand cases it is mere thirst to be assuaged : and who does not know that in hot summer days about the hardest thing for a laborer or traveller to get is a drink of water, pure, sparkling, dripping, cold ; the very sight of which bathes and refreshes the panting body and cools the hot blood.

Half of the Widow's Mite.

A gentleman called upon a rich friend for some charity.

"Yes, I must give you my mite," said the rich man.

"Do you mean the widow's mite ?" asked the solicitor.

"Certainly," was the answer.

"I shall be satisfied with half as much as she gave," said his friend. "How much are you worth ?"

"Seventy thousand dollars."

"Give me then your check for thirty-five thousand, that will be half as much as the widow gave ; for she, you know, gave her *all*."

The rich man was cornered. Covetous people often try to shelter themselves behind the widow's mite, and under the cover of her contribution give meanly to the Redeemer's cause. Her example indeed, rightly interpreted, would pluck selfishness out of the soul, and fill to overflowing the channels of true benevolence.

A Searching Test.

Worldliness is a more decisive proof of a low spiritual state than open sin ; for this may be sudden, the result of temptation, without premeditation, yet afterwards hated, repented of, repudiated, forsaken.

But if a man be *at home* in the world's pleasures and pursuits, content that his spirit should have no other heaven but in these things, happy if they could but last for ever, are not his state, genealogy, and character clearly stamped ?

Therefore does St. John draw the distinction : "If any man sin, we have an Advocate with the Father ;" but "If any man love the world, the love of the Father is not in him."

It is a rudeness among men to ask a favor, and not stay for an answer ; and do we count it no fault to pray for blessings, and never to think of them afterwards, never to wait for them, never to give God thanks for them ?

"THE sea is His, and He made it." How is the sea His more than the land? The land is cut up and divided off into farms and pastures and wood-lots and orchards and gardens; and these are owned and bought and sold, and descend to heirs in the line of many generations. And we build on them, and sow and reap and mow, and gather into storehouse and barn the fruits and grains of the land we enter on and possess. Their boundaries are carefully fenced off; rails and stones and wire define limits which all men respect, and each one is master of his own.

Not so the sea. Nobody dares claim an inch of the open sea. We cannot measure or partition its shining expanse. We cannot build our house or pitch our tents on its restless bosom. You may have a hut, or know the owner of one, on the mountain side. You see a light half way up its ascent in the evening, and you know there is a home and you might share it. The forests give their lost children berries and water; the sea mocks their thirst, and lets them die. We cannot so much as put a *stop* on its resistless flow. There is no rest on its billowy wastes. The bravest ship and the proudest fleet are at its mercy. Who can say but the next storm may sweep them for ever from our sight. And we can raise no tombstone and build no monument to the dead on its tossing waves. The sea drowns out humanity and time. It is an emblem of eternity, and of that it sings unceasingly. God will not share its dominion with man. "The sea is his, and he made it."

"Only just Inside the Fence."

"Oh," cried the little children—"Oh, such beautiful flowers, and only just inside the fence;" and then stealthy glances were cast up at the windows, the gate pressed softly, the beautiful flowers were snatched with a trembling hand, and the little ones fled away with beating hearts.

Only a little way had they gone, and lo, they had fallen into sin. Poor weak children we are all. Forbidden pleasures smile and beckon us "*only* just inside the fence." Our longing glances linger there; our feet enter in; it is a little way; no one sees us, and we put forth our hands and pluck the flowers whose fatal beauty is a snare to the soul. "Only just within the fence;" but within that fence is *sin*, without it is *safety*.

Change of Times.

In the annals of East Hampton, Long Island, not a century ago, we find the minister's salary forty-five pounds, lands rate free, grain to be first ground at the mill every Monday, and one-fourth the proceeds of the whales stranded on the beach.

Another little private
　　Mustered in
The army of temptation
　　And of sin.

Another soldier arming
　　For the strife,
To fight the toilsome battles
　　Of a life.

Another little sentry,
　　Who shall stand
On guard while evils prowl
　　On every hand.

Lord, our little darling
　　Guide and save,
'Mid the perils of the march
　　To the grave.

"THAT will break a proud man's heart which will scarcely break a humble man's sleep;" so true is it that many of the troubles of life affect our peace almost in the exact proportion to our pride or humility.

Good for Something.

The little mosses need not envy the hardy oak, the stately pine, or the scent-bearing magnolia, for they have their uses in the great universe of God, where not the smallest atom is in vain. The mosses not only clothe sterility, and beautify the waste with their clinging tendrils, but afford refuge in winter, and food as well as lodging in summer, to innumerable insects.

Overspreading the trunks and roots of trees, in winter they defend them against frost, in summer from the burning rays of the sun, and during the greatest drought provide them with moisture. Indeed to travellers in the dense and trackless forests of the North, they are pretty sure guides to the points of the compass, growing chiefly upon the north sides of the trees, as if to shelter them from the cold; in reality, because there the mosses find what they most need, shade and moisture.

The poor Laplanders find many comforts in the mosses. The Golden Maiden-hair makes excellent beds and coverlets. These are so elastic, that they can be rolled up and carried under the arm, and thus the people take them about on their journeys. In another softer moss the babies are wrapped up. They look much like little birds in their warm nests. The Greenlanders used moss for tinder and wicks of lamps.

The Precious Something.

A man tottering, not so much with age as with infirmity, passed a group of young men in the strength and freshness of early manhood. They were attracted by his pallor and feebleness, and words of pity fell from their lips.

"He does not need your pity," said one of the number; "that sick old man is a thousand times happier and a thousand times better off than you are."

"How so?" asked one, not without surprise.

"Because he has something that not only makes him happy in old age, and in pain and sickness, but which takes away the fear of death, and will carry him straight to heaven when he dies. No, he don't need our pity; he has true religion in his soul."

Such is the verdict of the world, in its sober moments, upon the believer's possession. And has he not indeed something more precious than gold, health, youth, any thing which this natural life has to offer—a hope, a joy, an inheritance which "fadeth not away," when every thing else fades?

THE bread-fruit tree is one of those wonderful sources of food which show the paternal care of God. It forms the chief support of the people of some of the South Sea Islands, where little else, either of vegetable or animal life, is found to eat. The tree grows to the height of forty feet or more. Its fruit is a large green berry, like a melon in form and size, and is in the greatest perfection about a week before it ripens. It is soft, tender, and white, resembling crumbs of bread; and it must be eaten while fresh, or it becomes hard and chokey. The flavor is like that of a roasted potatoe. It is usually cut into several pieces, and baked in an oven in the ground. It is a nice dish broken into orange juice or cocoa-nut milk.

It has been introduced into Madagascar and Mauritius, and shares with rice the favor of the natives. It has also been brought into the West Indies, and is taking root on our continent.

The Faith which Saves.

Just as you count "the seven springs" to be the Thames, *without* a flood of water, and without the navy that rides on the Thames; and just as you call the sapling an oak, without acorns; so God reckons the trust in him as righteousness, because it is the fountain and the root of righteousness, being indeed the divine life in the soul. But then that faith will *not be* without works, for the fountain *must* flow on, and the tree *must* grow, and the life of God in the soul *must* spring up into acts.

St. Paul says, Works are not enough to justify us, because they are limited and imperfect. True, replies St. James; but then do not think St. Paul means to say that a living fount of faith will be *barren*, without works. The faith which saves is not that kind which has no fruits, but that kind which is ever prolific—"a well of water springing up into everlasting life."   Robertson.

Beauty and Ugliness.

If we could but read it, every human being carries his life in his face, and is good-looking, or the reverse, as that life has been good or evil. On our features the fine chisels of thought and emotion are eternally at work. Beauty is not the monopoly of youth. There is a slow-growing beauty, which only comes to perfection in old age. Grace belongs to no one period of life, and goodness improves by age. I have seen sweeter smiles on the lip of seventy than I ever saw on the lip of seventeen. There is the beauty of youth, and there is also the beauty of holiness—a beauty much more seldom met, and more frequently found in the arm-chair by the fire, with grandchildren round its knee, than among the bustling cares and overanxious solicitudes of earlier days.

Consequences.

"Consequences! who cares for consequences?" cried a fast young man in answer to the advice and warning of a friend. Whether we care for consequences or not, they are certain to care for us; as poor M—— found, when two years after he fled from the city overwhelmed

with debt, took passage to Australia, and died in a grog-shop. These
consequences are terrible reckoners. They dog the evil-doer by night,
and track him by day; they appear as swift witnesses against him in
moments most unexpected; and flee as he may, they drag him down,
down to a perdition from which there is no escape.

We *must* care for consequences.

Music

Gives pleasant employment during leisure hours. There are leisure
hours in every family—evenings, Saturday afternoons, Sabbaths, when

the time can be enlivened, improved, and made delightful by appro-
priate music. Besides, temptations come to the young, especially to
young men, during unemployed hours. It is then that the dull family
fireside is left for the club, the theatre, or the street corner, where vice
presents her allurements, and the unsuspecting are enticed to ruin.
Few things can make home more attractive than music. It cheers men
in duty. The mother's soft lullaby soothes the sick child. By it the
laborer lightens his toils, and the soldier marches to battle. By it care
is lightened, sorrow assuaged, and our thoughts are borne heavenward.
Vocal music should be made a branch of study in all our schools, and
rank in importance with spelling, the multiplication table, and the
writing-book.

IF some good things of lower worth,
    My heart is called on to resign,
Of all the gifts in heaven and earth,
    The best, the very best is mine :
The love of God in Christ made known—
    The love that is enough alone ;
My Father's love is all my own.

How not to Quarrel with our Lot.

"It is something," said one who struggled and suffered, "to feel
the deep, deep conviction, which has never failed me in the darkest
hours, that Christ has the key to the mysteries of life, and that they
are not insolvable ; and that the spirit of the cross is the condition
which will put any one in possession of the same key : 'Take my yoke
upon you, and you shall find rest for your souls.' It is much to know
this ; for knowing it, I feel it is foolish and unphilosophical to quarrel
with my lot, for my wisdom is to transmute my lot by meekness into
gold. With God I cannot quarrel, for I recognize the justice and
beauty of his conditions. It is a grand comfort to feel that God is
right, whatever or whoever else is wrong. I *feel* St. Paul's words,
'Let God be true, and every man a liar.'"

"Come."

There is not a shorter, more precious, more hopeful, more inviting
word in all the Bible than this one small word "come." It is indeed
the key-note of the gospel. To the weary and heavy-laden, "Come"
and find rest; to the thirsty and fainting, "Come," "come and drink ;"
"come and take the water of life *freely ;*" only *come.* Was ever so
much depending on a condition so simple ?

The Guest.

"Behold, I stand at the door, and knock : if any man hear my voice, and open the door, I will come in to him, and will sup with him, and he with me." REV. 3:20.

Speechless Sorrow sat with me ;
I was sighing wearily ; .
Lamp and fire were out, the rain
Wildly beat the window-pane.
In the dark we heard a knock,
And a hand was on the lock ;
One in waiting spoke to me,
    Saying sweetly,
" *I am come to sup with thee.*"

All my room was dark and damp :
"Sorrow," said I, " trim the lamp,
Light the fire, and cheer thy face ;
Set the guest-chair in its place."
And again I heard the knock ;
In the dark I found the lock :
"Enter ; I have turned the key ;
    Enter, stranger,
Who art come to sup with me."

Opening wide the door, he came,
But I could not speak his name ;
In the guest-chair took his place,
But I could not see his face.
When my cheerful fire was beaming,
When my little lamp was gleaming,
And the feast was spread for three,
    Lo, my *Master*
Was the Guest that supped with me.

                  HARRIET McEwen KIMBALL.

A Short Sermon.

Rev. Dr. Muhlenberg preached a sermon at the funeral of the late Robert B. Minturn, in these words of the prophet Micah : " He hath shown thee, O man, what is good : and what doth the Lord require of thee, but to do justly, and to love mercy, and to walk humbly with thy God ?" adding, " *So did he.*" What higher eulogy, or more touching appeal ?

GOD will accept your first attempts to serve him not as a perfect work, but as a beginning. The first little blades of wheat are as pleasant to the farmer's eyes as the whole field waving with grain.

Old-time Legislation.

The American Congress, during the war of Independence, and in one of its darkest periods, adopted the following resolutions, October 12, 1778:

"Whereas true religion and good morals are the only foundation of public liberty and happiness:

"*Resolved*, That it be, and it is hereby earnestly recommended to the several states to take the most effectual measures for the encouragement thereof, and for the suppressing theatrical entertainments, horse-racing, gaming, and such other diversions as are productive of idleness, dissipation, and a general depravity of principles and manners.

"Whereas frequenting playhouses and theatrical entertainments has a fatal tendency to divert the minds of the people from a due attention to the means necessary for the defence of the country and the preservation of their liberties:

"*Resolved*, That any person holding an office under the United States, who shall act, promote, encourage, or attend such plays, shall be deemed unworthy to hold such office, and shall be accordingly dismissed."

Who can reckon up the damage and loss that might have been saved to the country, if the principles involved in this legislation could have been enforced and acted on?

Common Paths.

It sometimes seems to us a poor thing to walk in these common paths wherein all are walking; yet these common paths are the paths in which blessings travel. They are the ways in which God is met. Welcoming and fulfilling the lowest duties which meet us there, we shall often be surprised to find that we have been unawares welcoming and entertaining angels.

SINCE, in the dying words of La Place, "The known is little, but the unknown is immense," and

"Since life can little more supply
Than just to look about us and to die,"

it is a question of paramount importance, how in this short period education can be made to conduce most to the progress, the efficiency, the virtue, and the real welfare of man.

THE mind has more room in it than most people think, if you would but furnish the apartments.

Health

Is undoubtedly a great blessing ; but the world is full of the triumphs of soul over physical weakness and bodily infirmity : Paul, in "bodily presence weak ;" Timothy, "with his often infirmities ;" Baxter, never robust, often failing ; Milton, blind ; Payson, the victim of acute suffering ; Johnson, bravely carrying the weight of a diseased body ; Martyn, weak and worn ; Adolphe Monod, uttering under the pressure of torturing disease words that will be a power among men in other lands and future times. If sound health has its advantages, so has it its temptations ; and if ill health has its disabilities, so also it has its benefits. Though the outward man perish, the inward man may be renewed day by day, and shine with an ever-increasing clearness and lustre.

Nothing to Hold on by.

An infidel on his death-bed felt himself adrift in the terrible surges of doubt and uncertainty. Some of his friends urged him to hold on to the end.

"I have no objection to holding on," was the poor man's answer ; "but will you tell me what I am to hold on by ?"

There is the fatal want. Infidelity furnishes neither anchor nor rope to the sinking soul. It gives nothing to hold on by.

A Great Secret Told in a few Words.

"How is it you contrive to buy books as you do ?" said one journeyman to another. "Why, you have a nice little library here. Besides, you always have money to give to every good object that comes along. How do you do it ? My wages are as good as yours, and I can't do it."

"I do not spend my earnings for cigars, for soda, or ale, or oysters, nor do I run up a bill at the stables," was the answer.

I do not think the command to live "as pilgrims and strangers" means "rejoice in nothing," but "be *careful* for nothing." God does not require of us to tremble and be afraid, as if we were living in a world without foundations ; but to trust, as those who live in a world founded on his word, and having the firm support of his loving will. When he wills, we know the whole universe will fold up and be changed ; but then we shall have the firm support of his arm, with nothing intervening, and that will be as well.

Children at Play.

"I never was so mortified in my life," said a mother, "as once when I overheard one of my little girls, a make-believe mother, scolding a doll word for word, and tone for tone, as I was scolding Tom the day before. It was certainly not a pleasing *reflection.*"

Yes, go to the children *at play*, if you want to learn what influences are really educating them, for they *act* out the impressions most strongly made on them. It is not the more positive forms of training which at first or most influentially tell upon their young minds, but our *unconscious selves*, our habitual looks, acts, tones, expressions, which, like the air they daily breathe, daily moulds and vitalizes them. If you want to understand your child, see him at play. What variety, what heartiness, what soul on the playground! How bounding, free, outspoken, for good or for evil. Two things about play.

1. Children can play on very small capital. A little girl had nothing to play with but two empty spools. She named them Anne and Jane ; and the endless diversity of character and conduct they took was marvellous. Those children are not the happiest which have the fullest baby-houses. The scantier the material, the more the mind draws upon itself, and its very activity becomes a spring of unfailing enjoyment.

2. Let children *make* what they want as far as can be. A box of tools, a ball of twine, and a shingle will *educate* more than a year's schooling. Our boys never enjoyed their *gift* of a checker-board—a glad surprise, quickly over—as we in our childhood enjoyed constructing one ; marking off the squares, papering them, hunting the wood-pile for a crow-stick, and sawing off the men, with all the necessary finish. It took days of most enjoyable work. Nor do our little girls enjoy their doll's bedstead as we did, who manufactured one. Give the constructive faculties room and opportunity, and your children have a perpetual fund of healthy excitement to draw on.   K.

The True Ancestors of a Republic.

It is better to be the founder of a great name than its disreputable survivor. When a marshall of France was reminded by others of the obscurity of his birth, he proudly replied, "I am my own ancestor." In this great and original country, which is now treading in the van of a new reformation, we have thousands yet untaught who are to become ancestors in fame, ancestors in fortune, ancestors in science, ancestors in virtue. May their descendants be worthy of them.

MORE are they that *drift* into evil, than deliberately steer towards it.

United States Government.

EXECUTIVE DEPARTMENT.

PRESIDENT OF THE UNITED STATES-------------ANDREW JOHNSON, of Tennessee.
VICE-PRESIDENT OF THE UNITED STATES--------LAFAYETTE S. FOSTER, of Connecticut.

CABINET.

SECRETARY OF STATE-------------------- ----------WILLIAM H. SEWARD, of New York.
SECRETARY OF THE TREASURY-------------------HUGH McCULLOCH, of Indiana,
SECRETARY OF THE INTERIOR-------------------ORVILLE H. BROWNING, of Illinois.
SECRETARY OF THE NAVY----------------------GIDEON WELLES, of Connecticut.
SECRETARY OF WAR----------------------- ------EDWIN M. STANTON, of Pennsylvania.
ATTORNEY-GENERAL -------------------------HENRY STANBERY, of Kentucky.
POSTMASTER-GENERAL ----------------------ALEX'R W. RANDALL, of Wisconsin.

JUDICIARY DEPARTMENT.

SUPREME COURT OF THE UNITED STATES.

CHIEF-JUSTICE ------------------------------SALMON P. CHASE, of Ohio.
ASSOCIATE JUSTICE------ ----------------------SAMUEL NELSON, of New York.
"   "   ----------------------------ROBERT C. GRIER, of Pennsylvania.
"   "   ----------------------------JAMES M. WAYNE, of Georgia.
"   "   ----------------------------NOAH H. SWAYNE, of Ohio.
"   "   ----------------------------SAMUEL H. MILLER, of Iowa.
"   "   ----------------------------DAVID DAVIS, of Illinois.
"   "   ----------------------------NATHAN CLIFFORD, of Maine.
"   "   ----------------------------STEPHEN J. FIELD, of California
"   "   -----------------------------

The Supreme Court holds one session annually at Washington, commencing on the first Monday in December.

CONGRESS.—The apportionment made by Congress March 4, 1862, under the census of 1860, increases the number of Representatives to 242. There are also 9 Delegates from the Territories, who deliberate, but have no vote. The Senators are 72 in number. Each Senator and Representative is allowed $10,000 compensation for each Congress, (two years,) deducting for absence. This is an increase of $2,000 yearly over previous rates; the mileage, however, has been reduced. The Thirty-ninth Congress terminates March 3, 1867.

THE POST-OFFICE DEPARTMENT.—The revenue of the Department for the year ending June 30, 1865, was $14,556,158, and its expenditures $13,694,728; the rate of increase being 17 per cent., and of expenditure 8 per cent., compared with the previous year. Postage stamps to the value of $12,099,787 were sold, also $724,135 worth of stamped envelopes, and $23,315 of stamped wrappers. It is estimated that 467,591,600 letters were conveyed in the mails in 1865, of which 2,352,424 were lost or destroyed; the number of dead letters was 4,368,087. There were 74,277 money-orders issued, of the value of $1,360,122. The revenues of the past fiscal year exceeded the highest annual receipts from all the states previous to the rebellion by $6,038,091. The average annual increase of the revenue for the last four years over the preceding four years was $3,533,845. The Postmaster-general thinks that in a few years letter postage may be reduced to the rate adopted by Great Britain.

POSTAL MONEY-ORDERS.—On August 2, 1866, 300 new money-order offices were added, making 700 such post-offices. The largest amount that can be sent by any one order is now $50. The fees also have been changed—the charge now being 10 cents on any order from $1 up to $20; and 25 cents for any order over $20.

OUR INDIAN POPULATION.—According to the best data in the possession of the Indian Department at Washington, there are now between 320,000 and 350,000 Indians within the limits of the United States, comprised in about seventy-five tribes, and occupying about a hundred localities.

ITEMS FROM THE CENSUS REPORTS.—In 1700 the entire population of the Anglo-American colonies was 262,000; in 1750, it was 1,000,000; in 1775, 2,389,300. In 1790 the population of the United States alone was 3,929,827; and in 1860, 31,443,321. Anticipated population in 1900, 107,000,000.

The unimproved lands of the United States, in 1860, amounted to 244,101,818 acres; improved lands, 163,110,720 acres; cash value of the whole estimated at $6,645,045,007.

Estimated product of our manufactures in 1860, $4,000,000,000.

Commercial railroads in the United States, 35,935 miles, costing $1,432,649,000.

City railroads, 402 miles, costing $14,862,840.

Slack-water canals and branches, 118, of which 68 cost $147,393,997.

Real and personal property estimated at $19,089,156,289.

Educational institutions reported, 113,006; teachers, 148,742; students, 5,417,880. Collegiate institutions, 445; students, 54,969. Churches, 54,000.

Newspapers, 4,051; circulation, 928,000,000 copies.

Revolutionary army, from 1775 to 1783, 231,791; vessels, 4.

In 1812, regulars 32,360, volunteers 6,000, militia 30,000; navy, 8 frigates and 170 gunboats. In 1815, 276 vessels, with 1,636 guns.

In March, 1865, we had 684 vessels of war, with 4,477 guns, many of them of large calibre; and the aggregate number of men raised for the Union armies was 2,688,000. If the Confederate forces be added, the grand total would be reached of 4,000,000 of men at arms—the largest force ever yet raised in any country or age of the world.

AMERICAN SHIPPING.—Before the war, the Stars and Stripes led the carrying trade of the world. Not only was there a larger tonnage afloat under our flag than under any other, but American ships had the preference for enterprise, speed, and care of cargo, which gave them the lead in every port and on every ocean. The entire tonnage of Great Britain in 1861 was 4,806,826 tons; and that of the United States, 5,539,813 tons. In the trade of this country we kept the lead without the assistance of discriminating legislation. During the five years ending with 1861, the carrying trade of New York amounted to $1,644,000,000, of which over $1,000,000,000 was done under the American flag, leaving but little more than half that amount for the flags of all other nations on the globe. With the advent of war there came a disastrous change. The few privateers fitted out in English ports, chiefly through the assistance of British capitalists, turned the scale against us, and almost the entire fleet of American vessels were forced to engage in the government service, lie idle at the dock, or transfer their ownership to a foreign flag. Thus in the four years which followed, out of $1,700,000,000 of foreign trade for the city of New York, less than $400,000,000 were done under the Stars and Stripes, while over $1,300,000,000 were carried under foreign flags. In 1865, the entire foreign commerce of New York was $429,100,229; of which $345,750,622 was in foreign ships, and only $83,349,607 in American ships. This is a humiliating and exasperating record; yet in these Fenian movements our government and people refused to retaliate, preferring the surer and better triumphs of peace.

PRESENT CONDITION OF OUR NAVY.—The Navy Register for 1866 gives the following particulars of the reduction of our naval force: Since the close of the war, 225 vessels have been disposed of by sale, and 13 have been lost. The number of vessels retained in the service is 318, of which 73 are laid up in ordinary, 63 are building at the different navy-yards, 15 are fitting out for sea service, 35 are under repair, and 89 are employed at various naval stations as tugs and despatch boats, or in the Ordnance Department. This leaves 94 vessels, of which 90 are attached to our squadrons, while four are employed as supply steamers. These vessels are distributed among the different squadrons as follows:

	Vessels.	Guns.		Vessels.	Guns.
European squadron	7	102	Gulf squadron	18	138
Brazilian "	9	102	Special service	7	128
East India "	5	51	Receiving ships	6	143
West India "	9	85	Supply steamers	4	23
Pacific "	20	221			
Atlantic "	9	74		94	1,066

Aggregate tonnage, 103,622, old measurement.

MODERN ARMAMENTS.—The Army and Navy (Eng.) Gazette remarks as follows upon the progress making in military armaments: "We are told that the fortifications which compelled Admiral Nunez, the destroyer of defenceless Valparaiso, to retire from before Callao, were not constructed of either stone or earth, but consisted of iron turrets of great thickness, mounted with guns which threw shot of the weight of 400 and 500 pounds. We must now admit that armor-plated ships, and especially those built upon the turret system, are more than a match for stone and earthen fortifications; while on the other hand, we have a case in point where iron turrets placed upon the land can bid defiance to the approach of even a fleet of iron-clads."

The same paper refers to important trials of heavy rifled artillery, which have been made in past months at a large cost to that government, and says the report "leads irresistibly to the conclusion that in no system of grooved rifling at present known is the endurance of guns of large calibre fired with full charges of powder any thing more than a very limited quantity."

AMERICAN IRON-CLADS.—The sea-going qualities of vessels of the monitor class have been triumphantly tested by their safe passage across the ocean to England, and around Cape Horn to San Francisco. Their progress was remarkably uniform from day to day; and they proved very buoyant, and indifferent to storms. Admiral Porter says, in a report after the capture of fort Fisher, "The Monadnock," a double-turreted monitor of four guns, "could destroy any vessel in the French or British navy, lay their towns under contribution, and return again—provided she could pick up coal—without fear of being followed. She certainly could clear any harbor on our coast of blockaders, in case we were at war with a foreign power." The Monadnock attracted great attention in Europe, where her remarkable superiority, both for attack and defence, was generally conceded.

LOSSES OF THE NORTHERN ARMIES.—The Provost Marshal-general has compiled a complete list of all the deaths in battle and from wounds and disease, of every regiment from all the Northern states during the war. This record shows that 280,751 officers and men lost their lives in the service; of whom 5,221 commissioned officers and 90,886 enlisted men were killed in action or died of wounds, and 2,321 commissioned officers and 182,329 men died of disease.

THE CHARITIES OF THE WAR.—A careful statement made of the amount contributed by the people of the loyal states for philanthropic purposes connected with the war, not including the donations for religious or educational objects, gives the following noble record: The total contributions from states, counties, and towns for the aid and relief of soldiers amounted to $187,269,6 8 62; the contributions of associations and individuals for the care and comfort of soldiers, were $24,044,865 96; for sufferers abroad, $389,040 74; for sufferers by the riots of July, for freedmen and white refugees, $639,633 13: making a grand total, exclusive of expenditures of the government, of $212,274,248 45.

MORTALITY IN WAR.—From the report made to the late Statistical Congress at Berlin, by E. B. Elliot, representing our Sanitary Commission, it appears that the deaths in our army in the late civil war averaged 72 in each 1,000 every year; of which only 20 died in battle or of wounds, and 52 from disease or other causes. The ordinary mortality at the same age in civil life is 9 or 10 in 1,000; and of soldiers in peace, 26 in 1,000. The proportion of officers killed in battle is larger than of soldiers; but twice as many privates in proportion die of disease.

During Wellington's campaign in Spain, his army lost at the rate of 160 in 1,000 annually; and in the Crimean war, the mortality in the hospitals alone was 230 in 1,000, besides those who died in battle. Our soldiers in general were of better material than those in Europe, both physically and morally.

The latest military reports of Europe show that it has an aggregate of nearly 5,000,000 men under arms in time of peace; about one in 65 of the entire population, and one in 20 of the adult male population, a proportion greatly increased in time of war. But in our late war the North had not over one in 50 of its entire population in the field, or one in 24 of its adult males. Meanwhile our population went on increasing, and there were 150,000 more voters after the war than before.

NATIONAL DEBTS.—Mr. Gladstone's estimates.

England	----$3,995,000,000,	or $125 per head.	Spain	------	----$725,000,000,	or $46 per head.
Unit. States	3,000,000,000,	or 100 "	Holland	-------	425,000,000,	or 121 "
France	2,400,000,000,	or 53 "	Turkey	--------	255,000,000,	or 115 "
Austria	1,580,000,000,	or 45 "	Prussia	--------	215,000,000,	or 12 "
Russia	1,395,000,000,	or 43 "	Portugal	-------	175,000,000,	or 40 "
Italy	760,000,000,	or 34 "				

Great Britain's revenue has never exceeded $370,000,000 per year; but the United States government are now raising $540,000,000 per year.

RAILROAD TRAVEL IN NEW YORK.—On the eleven street railroads in the city of New York there were carried, during the year ending September 30, 1864, the enormous number of 60,328,795 passengers, exceeding that of the previous year by nearly 20,000,000. The earnings of the roads for the same period were $4,623,583, and the expenses $2,821,625.

CASUALTIES FOR 1865.—During the year 1865, there were 354 fires in the United States where the amount of loss was $20,000 or upwards, at which property was destroyed amounting, as estimated, to $43,139,000. The losses by fire from 1855 to 1865, inclusive, were $214,588,000. During the year there were 183 railroad accidents, by which 335 persons were killed and 1,427 wounded; and 32 steam-boat accidents, by which 1,788 were killed and 265 wounded. During the last twelve years there were 1,413 railroad accidents, by which 2,204 were killed and 8,356 wounded; and 324 steam-boat accidents, by which 6,372 were killed and 1,579 wounded.

DONATIONS TO COLLEGES.—During the last two years of the war, the very large sum of $818,000 was donated to New England colleges. The New England seminaries for young ladies meanwhile received less than a fiftieth part of the above noble subsidy.

REVOLUTIONARY PENSIONERS.—Congress has passed a bill giving a gratuity of $300 a year to each of the five surviving revolutionary pensioners, in addition to the pension of $100 which they now receive. In January, 1864, there were only twelve remaining, seven of whom have since died. The names of the only survivors are as follows: Lemuel Cook, enlisted in Hatfield, Mass., 98 years of age, now residing at Clarendon, Orleans county, New York; Samuel Downey, enlisted in Carroll county, New Hampshire, 98 years of age, now living at Edenburg, Saratoga county, New York; William Hutchins, enlisted in Newcastle, Maine, 100 years of age, residing at Penobscot, Maine; Alexander Maroney, enlisted at lake George, New York, as a drummer-boy, 94 years of age, residing at Yates, Orleans county, New York; James Beartham, a substitute for a drafted man in Southampton county, Virginia, living in Missouri, in his 101st year.

WORK OF THE BIBLE SOCIETY.—At the anniversary of the British and Foreign Bible Society, Viscount Stratford de Redcliffe referred to its marked accelerated progress, stating that he remembered that the first year the receipts were $3,200, while during the last year they amounted to nearly a million of dollars—$905,365. He also stated that forty-five million copies of the Scriptures had issued from the dépôts of the Society in the sixty years of its existence. While such a promulgation of the sacred word must have been accompanied by a great, a marked, and salutary improvement, he reminded the Society, as an incentive to still greater exertions, that their distribution, large as it was, could not have reached more than one-fifth of the 250,000,000 families in which the 1,200,000,000 of our fellow-creatures in the world are comprised.

AN AUSPICIOUS SIGN OF THE TIMES.—A wonderful movement is now in progress in France, for the purpose of securing a new translation of the Bible into French, none of the versions now in use being satisfactory. A Society has been formed, of which M. Thierry, a Senator and member of the Academy, is President, which held its first meeting March 21, 1866, when 2,000 persons were present. The movement originated with Rev. Mr. Petavel, pastor of the Swiss church in London, who has secured the enthusiastic aid of leading dignitaries and clergymen of the Protestant, Catholic, and Jewish faith, and of eminent men of all ranks. The translation is to be made by a committee of learned men from the three great religious communions. At the public meeting, addresses were made by Jewish rabbies and Catholic priests, heartily commending the object, and expressing the common desire that the word of God should be translated into their language with all possible accuracy and fidelity. A Catholic Abbé who disavowed the Inquisition, and rejoiced that the time had gone by when material constraint was needed to maintain any religious creed, mentioned as one of the desirable results of this translation, that it would establish an acknowledged authority in all religious controversies, and was destined to shed light upon disputed points. The decided support given to the measure by the Archbishop of Paris and by prominent Catholic clergymen has made a great sensation among extreme Romanists, who are using influences to induce them to withdraw.

SUBMARINE TUNNEL BETWEEN FRANCE AND ENGLAND.—A project which throws the famous Thames tunnel and all others completely in the shade—namely, the connecting of Dover and Calais by a submarine tunnel—is seriously entertained by the skilful engineers of France. The channel at that point is 26 miles across, and may be traversed without making artificial islands, by four galleries of little more than six miles each.

PRICES IN NEW YORK MARKET.—The following are the prices of leading articles in the New York market on January 3d, in each of the last six years, as prepared by the Commercial and Financial Chronicle:

	1861.	1862.	1863.	1864.	1865.	1866.
Ashes, pots, 100 lbs.	$5 00	$6 25	$8 50	$8 50	$11 75	$9 00
Pearls	5 00	6 25	8 25	9 75	13 00	11 00
BREADSTUFFS.						
Wheat Flour, State, per bbl.	5 35	5 50	6 05	7 00	10 00	8 75
Wheat, best extra Genesee	7 50	7 50	8 75	11 00	15 00	14 00
Rye Flour, "	4 00	3 87½	5 45	6 65	9 00	6 10
Corn Meal, Jersey	3 15	3 00	4 00	5 65	8 80	4 25
Wheat, white Genesee, bush.	1 45	1 50	1 60	1 80	2 60	2 63
Red Western	1 38	1 42	1 48	1 57	2 45	2 05
Rye, Northern, bush.	75	83	96	1 30	1 75	1 05
Oats, State	37	42	71	93	1 66	62
Corn, old Western	72	64	82	1 30	1 90	95
Cotton, mid. upland, lb.	12¼	35½	68½	82	1 20	52
Fish, dry Cod, qtl.	3 50	3 50	4 50	6 75	9 00	9 25
Fruit, bunch Raisins, box	1 75	3 20	3 50	4 00	5 85	4 40
Currants, lb.	4⅓	9	13a13½	15	21	15
Hay, shipping, 100 lbs.	90	77½	85	1 45	1 55	75
Hops, lb.	25	20	23	33	40	50
Iron, Scotch pig, ton	21 00	23 00	33 50	45 00	63 00	52 00
English, bars	52 00	57 00	77 50	90 00	190 00	130 00
Laths, per M.	1 30	1 25	1 45	1 50	2 40	5 00
Lead, Spanish, ton	5 25	7 00	8 00	10 50	15 00	10 00
Galena	5 50	7 12½	8 00	10 50	16 00	....
Leather, hemlock, sole, lb.	10½	20½	27	30	42	36
Oak	27	28	33	42	52	39
Lime, com. Rockland, bbl.	75	65	85	1 35	1 15	1 10
Liquors, Brandy, (cognac,) gal.	2 00	4 00	5 25	....	....	....
Domestic Whiskey	19¾	20½	39	94	2 24	2 27½
Molasses, New Orleans, gals.	37	53	55	70	1 43	1 15
NAVAL STORES.						
Spirits Turpentine, gal.	35	1 47½	2 60	2 95	2 10	1 05
Common Rosin, N. C., bbl.	1 25	6 00	10 50	30 00	28 00	6 50
Oils—Crude Whale, gal.	51	48	83	1 10	1 48	1 60
Crude Sperm	1 40	1 40	1 75	1 60	2 13	2 50
Linseed	50	86	1 27	1 47	1 50	1 45
PROVISIONS.						
Pork, old mess, bbl.	16 00	12 00	14 50	19 50	43 00	28 50
Pork, old prime	10 50	8 50	12 50	14 50	36 25	23 50
Beef, city mess	6 00	5 50	12 00	14 00	20 50	20 00
Beef Hams, extra	14 00	14 50	15 50	18 30	27 00	35 00
Hams, pickled, lb.	8	6	8	11	20	16½
Lard	10½	8⅝	10	13	23	19
Butter, Ohio	14	15	22	24	45	30
Butter, Orange county	22	22	25	32	63	50
Cheese	10	7	12	15½	20	18½
Rice, good, 100 lbs.	4 00	7 00	8 75	10 00	13 00	12 50
Salt, Liverpool, ground, sack	65	86	1 25	1 85	2 27	2 00
Liverpool, fine, Ashton's	1 60	1 70	2 15	2 80	4 75	4 10
Seeds, clover, lb.	8¾	7¼	10¾	12½	27	14
Sugar, Cuba, good	6¼	8¼	10	12	19	13
Tallow	9¾	9½	10⅜	12	18	14
Whalebone, Polar	88	76	1 65	1 60	2 25	1 55
Wool, fleece	30	50	60	75	95	75

FAILURES.—The following is a comparative statement of failures, their number, and amount, in 1865 and the previous nine years, in the Northern states:

	Number.	Liabilities.		Number.	Liabilities.
1857	4,257	$265,818,000	1862	1,652	$23,049,300
1858	3,113	73,608,747	1863	495	7,899.000
1859	2,959	51,314,000	1864	610	8,579,700
1860	2,733	61,739,474	1865	530	17,625,000
1861	5,935	178,632,170	Average from 1857 to 1865, 76,473,000.		

WANTS OF LARGE CITIES.—As a great city stretches its bounds on every side, it becomes more and more a necessity to provide ample, swift, and cheap conveyance for its vast population from side to side and to the suburbs. New York, for example, in addition to its grand system of ferries, must have a submarine tunnel connecting it with the opposite shores east and west. Nor can it long dispense with a far more ample and rapid mode of conveyance from its southern and business portions to its upper parts, and the towns beyond it on the north. It is proposed to construct a tunnel under the whole length of the city, from the Battery to the Central Park, to contain a double-track railway, on which steam cars can be run. This tunnel is to have numerous stations on the route, reached by staircases from the street. The expense will be about a million of dollars a mile. A light, airy, and pleasant road of this kind, five miles in length, has been built under the city of London, on which the cars travel at the rate of twenty miles an hour, with safety and comfort. At this rate cars could run from the Battery to the Central Park in twelve minutes.

DISPLAY OF THE WORLD'S INDUSTRY.—A "Universal Exposition of the Products of Industry and Art of all Nations" is to be held in Paris during the six months succeeding April 1, 1867. Its aim is to exhibit the progress of art and manufactures, and of all the sciences in supplying the necessities of society, among all the nations of the world. The government of France is to erect a palace for the Exhibition 1,600 feet long and 1,200 wide, covering an area of 35 acres, to cost $4,000,000 ; besides making provision for living products of agriculture and horticulture, animals, and models of villages. Compartments have been allotted to the Christian governments of Europe and America, and to the Mohammedan and Pagan nations of Turkey, Persia, Central and Southern Asia, China, Japan, Africa, and Oceanica. There will be a display of different races of savages at work in their rude industry.

ARTESIAN WELLS.—Paris having already two great artesian wells, another is being sunk. It has reached a depth of eighty-two metres, or 269 feet, nearly twenty-three metres below sea level. A good deal of difficulty has been experienced in dealing with a number of subterranean lakes met with.

CAPERNAUM.—Archæological searches in Palestine have nearly settled the site of ancient Capernaum upon the present Tel Hum. The "White Synagogue" has been dug out, and there is little doubt that this is the identical edifice built by the Roman centurion, Luke 7, and one of the structures in which Christ prayed and taught—the only one now to be traced. Its plan and ornaments have been made out and copied.

AN EGYPTIAN RELIC.—A stone has been discovered in Egypt, at ancient Tanis, which promises to be of almost equal value with the famous Rosetta stone. It contains a long inscription in the ancient hieroglyphics, with its counterpart in Greek; the whole in a most excellent state of preservation. It has already been three times photographed, and is ready for the labors of scholars.

AN AUSTRALIAN MONSTER.—An extraordinary reptile has arrived in England from Australia, which seems to be more nearly allied to the pre-Adamite Saurians than any thing before discovered. It possessed enormous claws and teeth, which enabled it to cause great destruction to the natives, while its almost impenetrable skin shielded it from their rude weapons. The body is perfect with the exception of one claw, torn off in the final contest.

PETROLEUM.—The demand for petroleum in Europe alone for the year 1866 is estimated at 90,000,000 gallons. The consumption in 1864 was 30,000,000 gallons, against 10,000,000 gallons in 1862. There is also a brisk demand for it in every country in the world that has learned the value of artificial light and of machinery.

FREE PUBLIC BATHS.—The city of Boston appropriated $10,000 for the erection of six bathing-houses in convenient locations, for the free use of the people. These are now opened, and in the warm weather are daily thronged. The swimming-rooms are each in the charge of a superintendent and policeman ; the water is four feet deep, and is kept pure by a constant current; and facilities for learning to swim are furnished. Similar conveniences ought to be furnished by every city and large town, as a public necessity.

Free Drinking Fountains also ought to be liberally provided, not only on the great highways and thoroughfares in the country, but at frequent intervals in every city. Pure and cool water in front of a corner grocery would draw away not a little of its custom.

NEW YORK STATE INEBRIATE ASYLUM.—Up to 1864, there had been 7,245 applications for places in this excellent institution at Binghamton, from every state in the Union, and from Europe, Mexico, and the British Provinces; 520 applicants were opium eaters. There were 39 clergymen, 8 judges, 197 lawyers, 226 physicians, 340 merchants, 680 mechanics, 466 farmers, 240 gentlemen, and 805 women. One of the opium eaters, a lawyer, who had filled a highly responsible office, in one year drank 3,200 bottles of McMunn's preparation of opium. In one day he drank twenty bottles, equal to ten thousand drops of laudanum. Patients at this asylum are received for not less than a year, are watched, controlled, and medically treated. The expectation is that at least seventy-five per cent. will be radically cured. The astounding fact was stated at a Temperance Convention at Saratoga, that the names of 1,300 rich men's daughters are on the list of applicants for admission to this asylum.

FAR-REACHING LIBERALITY.—Hon. Asa Parker of Mauch Chunk, Pennsylvania, has set apart five hundred thousand dollars to establish and endow a college near Bethlehem, giving also fifty-seven acres of land, on which the buildings will be erected, in which indigent boys shall have free education. This noble gift to the cause of education has not been surpassed in this country.

LONDON WATER.—The capital of England and many of its large towns are seriously troubled as to the impure quality of the water their people are compelled to use, which is found a fruitful source of disease. In *London*, the deep wells sunk under the city have been failing, the water level being 40 or 50 feet lower than 25 years ago, and it seems certain that no pumping process can supply the city. The immense expenditures for the sewerage of London and to purify the Thames water, do not alter the fact that there are 56 towns, with over 1,000,000 inhabitants, on the river above London, pouring their sewerage into the river. To remedy the frightful evils thus caused, an eminent engineer, Mr. Bateman, proposes a plan of relief, gigantic, but perhaps the only feasible one. This is to collect the waters from the mountain ranges of Northern Wales into artificial lakes, and convey them, by a series of aqueducts and reservoirs, to the city. The whole distance to the service reservoirs in London would be 183 miles; and the first cost of a supply of 130,000,000 gallons daily is estimated at $43,000,000. How to accomplish all this is a question; but a still graver question is, how to live without it. Meanwhile let us be grateful for our happy immunity from such perplexities at present, in our well-watered country.

THE GREAT AFRICAN DESERT.—Recent explorations have corrected many of the erroneous impressions respecting the great desert of Sahara. Instead of being a nearly level sandy plain, it is only so at its eastern and western extremities, the central portions rising in the form of terraces 900 or 1,200 feet above the valleys of the Atlas and Soudan, while Barth speaks of mountains 4,000 or 5,000 feet high. The opinion of Humboldt is undoubtedly correct, that it is the bed of a former sea elevated by geological convulsions, mounds of fossil shells and other debris of marine animals being met over its whole extent, besides immense deposits of rock salt. The fact has been revealed by numerous wells, that there are extensive sheets of water a short distance below the surface—a fact known for a long time to the Arabs, who call this watery bed the subterranean sea.

A WONDERFUL INCREASE.—The population of the state of Illinois has continued to increase beyond all precedent. In 1809 the territory of Illinois was constituted, and in 1818 the state was admitted into the Union. In 1820 its population was 55,211; in 1830 it was 157,445; in 1840, 476,183; in 1850, 851,470; in 1860, 1,711,951—an increase during the last decade of 860,481, or over 101 per cent., and in the last generation of thirty years of over 987 per cent.

COSMOPOLITAN CITIES.—The last English census developes the fact that there are in London more Scotchmen than in Edinburg, more Irish than in Dublin, more Roman-catholics than in Rome, and more Jews than in Palestine. New York has nearly as many Irish as Dublin, and is probably the third German city in the world, ranking next to Berlin and Vienna.

A GROWING POWER.—Since the days of Peter the Great, Russia has advanced her frontier 700 miles towards Vienna and Berlin, 500 miles towards Constantinople, and 1,200 miles towards Lahore and Kurrachee in India. She has taken from Sweden more than half her territory; from Poland, territory more extensive than Austria; from Turkey, provinces equal to Prussia and the Rhine provinces, Belgium, and Holland; from Persia, provinces as large as Great Britain; and from Tartary and China, countries greater than the whole of Europe. Her population in the same time has increased sixfold.

WASTING SOURCE OF ENGLAND'S STRENGTH.—The predominance of the commerce of Great Britain over that of America and France has been owing greatly to her vast resources of coal, covering an area of 5,400 square miles, and estimated to have been originally nearly 200,000,000,000 tuns. The people of that country are now startled by the statement, that such has been the drain, that probably one-half of the store has been consumed, and that the remainder will be exhausted in about a century. Mr. Gladstone and Stuart Mill have called the attention of Parliament to the matter in earnest and impressive speeches, for the purpose of urging them to take measures now for the reduction of their immense national debt.

THE ITALIAN PATRIOT'S OPINION.—Garibaldi, who has shown such an illustrious and dis-
interested devotion to the best interests of Italy, has written a letter intimating that he will
use all the agencies at his command to facilitate the circulation of the New Testament in
every part of Italy. After denouncing popery as the most colossal system of iniquity the
world ever saw, he expresses his deep conviction that nothing but the circulation of the New
Testament can ever effectually crush it in his native land. The anxiety for the possession
of copies of the New Testament is rapidly increasing in all parts of Italy.

JUVENILE REFORM SCHOOLS.—The first of these, the House of Refuge in New York, was
founded in 1824, and has now about 1,000 inmates. Then followed the Juvenile Asylum,
averaging 450 to 500, and having received in the last 14 years 12,000 children. Some 60 on
the average are received each month, and as many disposed of—usually to western farms,
2,000 having been sent to Illinois alone. Juvenile Reform schools are now established in
all the New England states, and in New Jersey, Pennsylvania, Ohio, Michigan, Illinois, Wisconsin, Kentucky, Missouri, Maryland, and Louisiana.

The Children's Aid Society in New York is a recent but very efficient laborer in this
important field. In the last year 1,400 homeless children were provided for by it, and in 13
years over 10,000 have been placed in good homes. About 20 "Industrial Schools" also add
their efforts, in teaching and otherwise caring for the poor children of New York. The
Children's Aid Society lately received from Chauncey Rose, Esq., a munificent gift, which
will yield them an income of $10,000 yearly.

JAPAN.—This empire is slowly opening to the better knowledge of foreigners, and admit-
ting their arts, sciences, and influence. An English paper is now published there, carriages
are introduced, and a railroad with engine and tender is in operation at Nagasaki, and excites
a great deal of attention, the Japanese coming from far and near to see it. The value of the
imports to Japan in 1864 was about $9,400,000; exports nearly $14,000,000. Nearly 200 vessels are annually entered and cleared, some 50 of them American.

The anti-foreign policy of the Japanese government is believed to have undergone an
important change for the better near the close of 1865, the united forces of the foreign powers having secured the revision of the tariff and the opening of two new ports, Osaka and
Hiogo, as well as the ratification of previous treaties by the Mikado. This official is found to
be the only real emperor, the Tycoon being only one of many Daimios, or hereditary princes,
though having some special privileges—being usually a son-in-law of the Mikado.

CHRISTIAN MISSIONS.—The enemies of religion have recently assailed the work of missions as a failure, affirming among other things that the great Societies are barely holding
their own by special exertions; that the missions have not advanced into new heathen territory; and that less actual progress has been made of late than in previous years. These
plausible charges have called out a public and full refutation by facts. Thus as to *receipts*,
it is shown that in 1854 the receipts from the prominent organizations in England and the
United States were $800,000; while in 1865 they were almost $1,400,000; an increase of 75
per cent. In the same period, their number of missionaries and helpers has increased from
679 to over 1,100. With regard to *new territory*, Japan has been partly occupied; the large
province of Pe-chih-li in China with 31,000,000 of people, and another province called Hapeb,
with 30,000,000. In India, two new states have been entered by the Methodist Episcopal
church of the United States; one new state by the Scotch United Presbyterians; the vast
territory of the Nizam is the scene of a new and great movement by the Church Missionary
Society, who have also just entered Cashmere. Many other minor advances have been made
in India, as well as in Burmah, Madagascar, Mauritius, and Egypt. Thus within 10 years
new ground has been occupied by 150 missionaries among a population of 150,000,000.
Finally, as to accessions to the church, a careful review of the whole ground proves that,
with scarcely an exception, the triumphs of the gospel have been greater in the last ten
years than ever before, and that in real efficiency and spiritual life, as well as numbers, the
missions were never so powerful as to-day.

In the various Protestant missionary fields, there are now some 1,200 ordained native
preachers, and over 6,000 other native helpers. In India, the very gratifying and suggestive
fact is disclosed, that of all the male converts, *one in seven* is employed in one form or another of mission work.

SUGGESTIVE COMPARISONS.—In 1839, there were connected with the missions of the
American Board 52 churches, with 7,311 members. There were then in Massachusetts 375
evangelical congregational churches, with 52,823 members. During the next 25 years,

55,480 members were added to the mission churches, and 55,766 to the churches in Massachusetts. The average number of mission churches for the whole time was 105; in Massachusetts, 452. The average yearly additions to each church in the mission, a little over 21; in Massachusetts not quite 5.

PROGRESS OF FREEDOM.—The present century has been signalized by the breaking of the fetters of the slave in most of the lands where man was held in bondage. In 1807 the slave-trade was suppressed by Great Britain, in 1808 by the United States, and in 1820 by France. In 1818 slavery was abolished by the Netherlands, in 1834 by Great Britain, in 1846–47 by Sweden, in 1848 by France and Denmark, in 1860–61 by Holland. In 1862 serfdom was abolished by Russia; in 1863 emancipation was proclaimed by President Lincoln; in 1865 it was promised by the king of Portugal. Spain and Brazil, the only remaining countries in Christendom where slavery is still established, have passed laws or are discussing measures looking to an early removal of the institution.

THE SINAITIC CODEX.—This is an ancient manuscript copy of the New Testament entire, found by Dr. Tischendorf, a most eminent German scholar, in the convent at mount Sinai. It is believed to be more ancient than the celebrated Vatican manuscript at Rome, which has never been thoroughly examined, and which lacks the book of Revelation and several of the Epistles. The Sinaitic manuscript contains essentially the text as it was in the second century, and furnishes invaluable aid towards securing the exact original as penned by the sacred writers.

TRUE SCIENCE NOT CONTRARY TO SCRIPTURE.—While infidels ridicule the faith of Christians, facts prove that there are none so credulous as they in seizing upon and accepting whatever in their opinion will discredit or overthrow the sacred record. An immense quantity of flints shaped like axes, arrow-heads, and other rude implements, found in the valley of the Somme, in Picardy, Northern France, led many geologists to pronounce that they afforded incontrovertible proof of the existence of man for ages before the creation of Adam, according to the Bible, though it is known that flint has a natural tendency to break into similar shapes. Some human bones and flint arrow-heads found last year in mounds at Caithness, in Scotland, were elaborately described, and authoritatively pronounced by scientific men to belong to a period before the Scripture record. A thorough investigation of the mounds, however, has proved them to be composed of limpets and periwinkle shells, and the human remains to be those of a Danish sailor, while a pair of tailor's shears like those in modern use, and coins bearing the image of King William III., were also found among these "pre-historic remains."

SCIENCE AGAINST HEATHENISM.—The fossilized forms of heathen superstition and idolatry are receiving ruthless blows from the improvements of modern science introduced by Christian civilization. In India, the railroads are fast destroying the restrictions of caste, which forbid men of different grades to associate. Travellers on the cars eat and drink, when they need refreshment, wherever they can obtain it. Instead of consulting astrologers when to start on a journey, they now go by railroad time. Pilgrims to the holy shrines, instead of measuring their lengths over the road, or painfully walking the distance, take the quickest route by rail. Instead of regarding it as pollution to touch a dead body, medical studies are eagerly pursued, and dissection is practised without scruple by men of the highest caste. Steam and the electric telegraph are doing much to demolish the decaying structure of Hinduism.

"AND A STRANGER THEY WILL NOT FOLLOW."—A man accused of stealing sheep was brought before a judge in India. As he could not decide between him and the supposed owner, both of whom had witnesses to prove their claims, he ordered the sheep to be brought into court, and sent one of the men into another room, while he told the other to call the sheep, and see if it would come to him. Not knowing the voice of a stranger, it would not go to him. In the meantime the other man, suspecting what was going on, gave a kind of "chuck," in the way he had been used to call the sheep, when it at once bounded towards the sound, thus deciding who was the real owner.

A VOLCANO IN THE SANDWICH ISLANDS.—Mauna Loa, a volcano in Hawaii, was the scene, at the opening of 1866, of a most sublime spectacle. A grand eruption commenced near the top of the mountain, and after pouring out its burning floods for two days, ceased; but 36 hours after the eruption again appeared, about midway on the mountain side, sending up a column of lava about 100 feet in diameter, varying from 100 to 1,000 feet in height, and continuing for twenty days and nights. The disgorgement from the mountain side was often with terrific explosions, which shook the hills and were heard for forty miles. This column of liquid fire was an object of surpassing brilliancy, of intense and awful grandeur. As the jet issued from the awful orifice, it was white heat; as it ascended higher and higher, it reddened like fresh blood, deepening its color, until, in its descent, much of it assumed the color of clotted gore.

In a few days it had raised a cone some three hundred feet high around the burning orifice, and as the showers of burning minerals fell in livid torrents upon the cone, it became one vast heap of glowing coals, flashing and quivering with restless action, and sending out the heat of ten thousand furnaces in full blast. The struggles in disgorging the fiery masses, the upward rush of the column, the force which raised it one thousand vertical feet, and the continuous falling back of thousands of tons of mineral fusia into the throat of the crater, and over a cone of glowing minerals one mile in circumference, was a sight to inspire awe and terror, attended with explosive shocks which seemed to rend the mural ribs of the mountain. From this fountain a river of fire went rushing and leaping down the mountain with amazing velocity, filling up basins and ravines, dashing over precipices, and exploding rocks, until it reached the forests at the base of the mountain, where it burned its fiery way, consuming the jungle, evaporating the water of the streams and pools, cutting down the trees, and sending up clouds of smoke and steam and murky columns of fleecy wreaths to heaven.

All Eastern Hawaii was a sheen of light, and night was turned into day. So great was the illumination at night, that one could read without a lamp; and labor, travelling, and recreation might go on as in the daytime. Mariners at sea saw the light at two hundred miles distance. It was a pyrotechnical display more magnificent and marvellous than was ever made by any earthly monarch. The point from which the fire-fountain issued is ten thousand feet above the level of the sea, thus making the igneous pillar a distinct object of observation along the whole eastern coast of Hawaii.

During the eruption, Rev. Mr. Coan made an excursion to the source. After three days of hard struggling in the jungle and over fields, ridges, and hills of bristling scoria, he arrived near sunset at the scene of action. All night long he stood as near to the glowing pillar as the vehement heat would allow, listening to the startling explosions and the awful roar of the molten column, as it rushed upward a thousand feet, and fell back in a fiery avalanche which made the mountain tremble. It was such a scene as few mortals ever witnessed. There was no sleep for the spectator. The fierce red glare, the subterraneous mutterings and strugglings, the rapid explosions of gases, the rushes and roarings, the sudden and startling bursts, as of crashing thunder—all, all were awe-inspiring, and all combined to render the scene one of indescribable brilliancy and of terrible sublimity. The rivers of fire from the fountain flowed about thirty-five miles, and stopped within ten miles of Hilo. Had the fountain played ten days longer, it would probably have reached the shore.

TORPEDOES.—Numerous experiments have been made in constructing, locating, and exploding these formidable implements, during previous wars and rumors of war; in general, with little success. Of late, however, they have been more skilfully made and used, sometimes with amazing effect, and more damage was done to national vessels by Southern torpedoes than by artillery, however excellent and well-served. They can be buried in the approaches to any fortified place, by land or by sea, and explode when struck by a passing ship, or by electricity, at any desired instant, by means of wires. They will evidently form a most important implement in future wars.

THE METRIC OR DECIMAL SYSTEM of weights and measures, adopted years ago in France, is gaining ground in Europe, and was unanimously approved by the British Association for the Advancement of Science in 1864, for universal adoption; and numerous means were recommended to bring it to the familiar knowledge of the people. In the debate on this subject, it was stated that, at a recent Postal Congress at Paris, where sixteen governments of Europe and America were represented, a resolution was unanimously adopted in favor of a universal metric postal system; that the discordant systems of weights and measures in different countries make the science of one nation almost a sealed book to others; that a boy taught arithmetic on the metric system, could make as much progress in ten months as in two years and ten months of study by the old systems; that the decimal system prevails throughout China, and was there believed to be of heavenly origin. So strong are the reasons for the proposed change, that it will doubtless in time be made, the new method being introduced in schools and in books, and gradually finding its way to popular favor and universal adoption.

The *meter* is the principal and only unit. It is a measure of length, and was intended to be one ten-millionth of the distance on the earth's surface from the equator to the pole. It is 39 inches and 37 one-hundredths very nearly.

The *are* is a surface equal to a square whose side is ten meters. It is nearly four square rods.

The *liter* is the unit for measuring capacity, and is equal to the contents of a cube whose edge is a tenth part of the meter. It is a little more than a wine quart.

The *gram* is the unit of weight, and is the weight of a cube of water, each edge of the cube being one one-hundredth part of the meter. It is equal to 15 grains and 432 one-thousandths.

The *stere* is a cubic meter.

Each of these units is divided decimally, and larger units are formed by multiples of ten, one hundred, etc. The successive multiples are designated by the prefixes, deka, hecto, kilo, and myra; the parts by deci, centi, and milli.

The nomenclature, simple as it is in theory, and designed from its origin to be universal, can only become familiar by use.

Like all strange words, these will become familiar by custom, and obtain popular abbreviations. A system which has incorporated with itself so many different sizes of weights, and such a nomenclature as scruples, pennyweights, "avoirdupois," and with no invariable component, can hardly prevail against a nomenclature whose leading characteristic is a short component word, with a prefix signifying number.

A Committee of Congress, to whom this matter was referred, reported unanimously in favor of the metric system, and recommended the passage of a law to legalize it, without at once substituting it for our present system.

After answering every argument for a change of nomenclature, the committee came to the conclusion that any attempt to conform it to ours in present use would lead to confusion, and would seriously interfere with the universality of a system so essential to international and commercial intercourse.

The committee unanimously recommended the enactment of the bill and accompanying resolutions reported by them. They were not prepared to go at this time beyond this stage of progress in the proposed reform. The metric system is already used in some arts and trades in this country, and is especially adapted to the wants of others. Its minute and exact divisions specially adapt it to the use of chemists, apothecaries, the finer specimens of the artisan, and to all scientific objects. Yet in some of the states, owing to the phraseology of their laws, it would be a direct violation of them to use it in the business transactions of the community. It is therefore very important to legalize its use, and give to the people, or that portion of them desiring it, the opportunity of its legal employment, while the knowledge of its characteristics will be thus diffused among men. When its convenience is manifest, a further act of Congress can fix the date for its exclusive adoption as a legal system. At an earlier period it may introduce it into all public offices and for government services.

FORM OF A BEQUEST.—I bequeath to my executors the sum of ---------------dollars, *in trust*, to pay over the same in ----------after my decease, to the person who, when the same is payable, shall act as treasurer of the------------Society, formed in----------in the year eighteen hundred and---------to be applied to the charitable purposes of said Society, and under its direction.

TABLE OF SIMPLE INTEREST AT SIX PER CENT.—

Principal.	One Mo'th			One Year.			Principal.	One Month.			One Year.			Principal.	One Month.			One Year.		
	D.	C.	M.	D.	C.	M.		D.	C.	M.	D.	C.	M.		D.	C.	M.	D.	C.	M.
Cents 10	0	0	0	0	0	6	Dolls. 6	0	3	0	0	36	0	Dolls. 40	0	20	0	2	40	0
" 50	0	0	2	0	3	0	" 7	0	3	5	0	42	0	" 50	0	25	0	3	00	0
Dolls. 1	0	0	5	0	6	0	" 8	0	4	0	0	48	0	" 60	0	30	0	3	60	0
" 2	0	1	0	0	12	0	" 9	0	4	5	0	54	0	" 70	0	35	0	4	20	0
" 3	0	1	5	0	18	0	" 10	0	5	0	0	60	0	" 80	0	40	0	4	80	0
" 4	0	2	0	0	24	0	" 20	0	10	0	1	20	0	" 90	0	45	0	5	40	0
" 5	0	2	5	0	30	0	" 30	0	15	0	1	80	0	" 100	0	50	0	6	00	0

The interest of any sum in *dollars* for 6 days, is the same sum in *mills:* namely, of $100, 100 mills, or 10 cents; of $6,600, 6,600 mills, or $6 60, etc. Money at compound interest will double itself in 11 years, 10 months, and 22 days.

ANNIVERSARIES AND OFFICERS OF CHARITABLE SOCIETIES, ETC.

BOSTON.—AM. BOARD FOR FOR. MISSIONS, 1st Tues, in Oct.; Rev. Rufus Anderson, D. D., Rev. Selah B. Treat, Rev. Nathaniel G. Clark, Sec's ; Langdon S. Ward, Treas., Miss. house, 33 Pemberton-square ; Rev. Geo. W. Wood, Sec. in New York, Bible-house. AM. BAP. MISS. UNION, 4th Tues. in May ; Rev. Jos. G. Warren, D. D., Sec.; Rev. J. N. Murdock, D. D., Assist. Sec.; F. A. Smith, Treas., 12 Bedford-st. AM. ED. SOC., in May ; Rev. I, N. Tarbox, Sec.; S. T. Farwell, Treas., 15 Cornhill. AM. TRACT SOC. (national) N. E. BRANCH ; G. Punchard, Sec., N. P. Kemp, Treas., 40 Cornhill. AMER. TRACT SOC. AT BOSTON. last Wed. in May ; Rev. W. C. Childs, D. D., Rev. I. P. Warren, Sec's ; Henry Hill, Treas., 28 Cornhill. MASS. HOME MISS. SOC., Rev. H. B. Hooker, D. D., Sec., Cong'l Lib. MASS. S.-S. SOC., Rev. A. Bullard, Sec., H. M. Sargent, Treas., 13 Cornhill. AM. S.-S. UNION, H. D. Noyes, Agt., 117 Washington-st.

NEW YORK.—AM. BIBLE SOC., 2d Thurs. in May ; Rev. Jos. Holdich, D. D., Rev. W. J. R. Taylor, D. D., Sec's ; Caleb T. Rowe, General Agent ; Henry Fisher, Assist. Treas., Bible-house, Astor-place. AM. AND FOR. BID. SOC., U. D. Ward, Cor. Sec., George Gault, Treas., 116 Nassau-st. AM. BIBLE UNION, Wm. H. Wyckoff, LL. D., Cor. Sec., Rev. C. A. Buckbee, Asst. Treas., 350 Broome-st. AM. TRACT SOC., Wed. preced. 2d Thurs. in May ; Rev. Wm. A. Hallock, D. D., Rev. O. Eastman, Rev. J. M. Stevenson, D. D., Cor. Sec's ; O. R. Kings-bury, Assist. Sec. and Treas., 150 Nassau-st. AM. HOME MISS. SOC., Wed. preced. 2d Thurs. in May ; Rev. Milton Badger, D. D., Rev. David B. Coe, D. D., Rev. A. H. Clapp, Cor. Sec's ; C. R. Robert, Treas., Bible-house, Astor-place. AM. BAP. HOME MISS. SOC., Rev. J. S. Backus, D. D., Sec.; J. M. Whitehead, Assist. Treas., 39 Park Row. BOARD OF FOR. MISS. OF PRES. CHURCH, Hon. Walter Lowrie, Rev. John C. Lowrie, D. D., Rev. David Irving, Cor. Sec's ; Wm. Rankin, Jr., Treas., 23 Centre-st. AMER. AND FOR. CHRIS. UNION, Tues. preced. 2d Thurs. in May ; Rev. Joseph Scudder, Rev. A. E. Campbell, D. D., Albert Woodruff, Sec's ; T. S. Young, Treas., 156 Chambers-st. AM. SEAMEN'S FRIEND SOC., Monday preced. 2d Thurs. in May : Rev. H. Loomis, Sec.; S. Brown, Assist. Treas., 80 Wall-st. NATIONAL TEMP. SOCIETY, Rev. L. D. Barrows, D. D., Cor. Sec., 172 William-st. PROTESTANT EPIS. CHURCH MISSION—Domestic Committee, Rev. J. D. Carder, D. D., Sec. and General Agent, 17 Bible-house ; For. Com., Rev. S. D. Denison, Sec., 19 Bible-house. EVAN. KNOWLEDGE SOC., Rev. H. Dyer, D. D., 3 Bible-house. METH.—Book Concern, T. Carlton, D. D., and J. Porter, D. D., Agents, 200 Mulberry-st.; Mission. Soc., J. P. Durbin, D. D., Cor. Sec., T. Carlton, D. D., Treas., 200 Mulberry-st.; S. S. Union, D. Wise, D. D., Cor. Sec.; Tract Soc. Meth. Epis. Ch., J. Porter, D. D., Treas.; Rev. D. Wise, D. D., Cor. Sec., 200 Mulberry-st. REF. DUTCH—Dom. Mission, Rev. G. Talmage, Cor. Sec., 103 Fulton-st.; Board of Pub., Wm. Ferris, Agent and Sec., Peter Duryee, Treas., 215 Greenwich-st.; Foreign Mission, Rev. J. M. Ferris, Cor. Sec., 103 Fulton-st., G. G. Smith, Treas. Board of Education, Rev. John L. See, Cor. Sec., 103 Fulton-st. SOC. FOR COL. AND THEOL. EDUCA. AT WEST, Rev. T. Baldwin, Sec., 42 Bible-house. AM. MISS. ASSO., Rev. George Whipple, and Rev. M. E. Strieby, Sec's ; L. Tappan, Treas., 61 John-st. N. Y. STATE COLON. SOC., Rev. J. B. Pinney, LL. D., Cor. Sec., 22 Bible-house. N. Y. S.-S. UNION, —— —— Agent, 599 Broadway ; and AM. S.-S. UNION, Rev. S. B. S. Bissell, Sec., G. S. Scofield, Agent, 599 Broadway. NEW YORK SAB. COM., Rev. Philip Schaff, D. D., Sec., 5 Bible-house.

PHILADELPHIA.—PENN. BRANCH AM. TRACT SOC., 1210 Chestnut-st., H. N. Thissell, Agent and Supt. Colp. AM. S.-S. UNION, F. A. Packard, Esq., Cor. Sec., 1122 Chestnut-st. GEN. ASSEM. BOARDS—Domestic Missions, 9'0 Arch-st., T. L. Janeway, D. D., Cor. Sec.; S. D. Powel, Esq., Treas. Education, 821 Chestnut-st., Rev. Thomas McCauley, Sec.; William Main, Treas. Publication, 821 Chestnut-st., Wm. E. Schenck, D. D., Cor. Sec. and Editor ; Winthrop Sargent, Super. of Colp., and Treas. AM. BAP. PUBLICA. SOC., 530 Arch-st.; Rev. B. Griffiths, Cor. Sec. PENN. BIBLE SOC., 701 Walnut-st., Jos. H. Dulles, Cor. Sec. PHILA. EDUCA. SOC., Charles Brown, Cor. Sec.; William Purves, Treas., 1334 Chestnut-st. PHILA. HOME MISSION SOCIETY, Rev. Robert Adair, Sec., 1334 Chestnut-st. LUTHERAN BOARD OF PUB., 42 North Ninth-st., Rev. Samuel Laird, Cor. Sec. PRES. PUB. COM., 1334 Chest-nut-st., Rev. John W. Dulles, Cor. Sec.; Wm. L. Hildeburn, Treas. DOM. MISS. GER. REF. CHURCH, 493 N. 4th-st.; Rev. S. H. Giesy, Cor. Sec. FOR. MISS. REF. PRES. CHURCH, 636 North 17th-st.; Rev. S. O. Wylie, Chairman.

WASHINGTON.—AMERICAN COLONIZATION SOCIETY, 3d Tues. in Jan.; Rev. R. R. Gurley, Cor. Sec.; Rev. Wm. McLain, Fin. Sec.

MINISTERS' MEETINGS.—GEN. CONFERENCE IN MAINE, 3d Tues. in June. GEN. ASSO., NEW HAMPSHIRE, 4th Tues. in Aug. GEN. CONVEN. IN VERMONT, 3d Tues. in June. GEN. ASSOCIA., MASS., 4th Tues. in June. EVAN. CONSO., R. I., 2d Tues. in June. GEN. ASSO., CONN., 3d Tues. in June. GEN. ASSO., N. Y., 3d Tues. in Sept. GEN. CONVEN. PROT. EPIS. CH., 1st Wed. in Oct. GEN. ASSEMBLY PRES. CHURCH, 3d Thurs. in May. GEN. CONFER. M. E. CHURCH, May every 4th year from 1860. GEN. SYNOD REF. DUTCH CHURCH, on the 1st Wed. in June. GEN. SYNOD EVANG. LUTHERAN CHURCH, biennially in May of even years.

YEARLY MEETINGS OF FRIENDS.—NEW ENGLAND, Newport, R. I. Second day after 2d Sixth day in Sixth mo. NEW YORK, Sixth day after 4th First day in Fifth mo. PHIL., third Second day in Fourth mo. BALTIMORE, last Second day but one in Tenth mo. NORTH CAROLINA, New Garden, Guilford Co., Second day after first First day in Eleventh mo; OHIO, Mt. Pleasant, Second day after first First day in Ninth mo. INDIANA, Whitewater, on Fifth day preced. first First day in Tenth month.

NEW AND ATTRACTIVE PUBLICATIONS.
American Tract Society,
150 NASSAU-STREET, NEW YORK.

LIFE AND TIMES OF JOHN MILTON. Steel portrait.
LIFE AND TIMES OF MARTIN LUTHER. Steel portrait.
THE AWAKENING IN ITALY, AND THE CRISIS OF ROME.
RECORDS FROM THE LIFE OF S. V. S. WILDER, including sixteen years in Paris; of almost romantic interest to the merchant, the civilian, and the Christian. Steel portrait. $1; morocco extra, $3 50.
THE YOUNG LADY OF PLEASURE. By an accomplished teacher of youth. Frontispiece in tint. Chaste and beautiful in style, containing invaluable suggestions on home duties and relations, and the chief matters of interest in a young lady's life. $1.
VITAL GODLINESS. By Rev. William S. Plumer, D. D. A valuable treatise on the great themes of experimental and practical religion. $1.
JOHN VINE HALL, or Hope for the Hopeless. One of the best temperance works of the age. Steel portrait. 60 cts.

BEAUTIFULLY ILLUSTRATED BOOKS FOR THE YOUNG.
SQUARE 16MO.
SISTERS, AND NOT SISTERS. An impressive exhibition of the results of performing and of neglecting sisterly duties. 75 cts.
LYNTONVILLE, OR THE IRISH BOY IN CANADA. A fresh picture of life in the new settlements in Canada. 60 cts.
AMONG THE WILLOWS. The happy influence of self-denying effort among the neglected. 50 cts.
THE CLIMBERS. An inspiriting book for boys.
PHIL KENNEDY. Illustrating the care of Providence.
HOURS WITH MAMMA. Forty fine engravings. Home talks about Bible heroes and scenes.
GRACE'S VISIT. A delightful record of Christian fidelity triumphant.
SYBIL GREY. Her visit to the city. An excellent book for young ladies.
OUR SYMPATHIZING HIGH-PRIEST. By A. L. O. E. 30 cts.
VOLUMES 18MO.
THE GLEN CABIN. Exciting scenes among the White Hills. 50 cts.
LILIAN. A tale of three hundred years ago. 50 cts.
THE HUGUENOTS OF FRANCE, or the Times of Henry IV. 50 cts.
EVELYN PERCIVAL. Highly interesting sketches, drawn from life. 50 cts.
ILVERTON RECTORY, or the Non-conformists of the 17th Century. 50 cts.
GREEN PASTURES, for the Lambs of Christ's Flock. 50 cts.
CLAYTON ALLYN. The trials and triumphs of an orphan lad. 50 cts.
SAVE THE ERRING, or the Gospel Purpose. A pleasing narrative. 40 cts.
EFFIE MORISON, or the Family of Redbraes. A narrative of truth. 40 cts.
WHILE THEY ARE WITH US. A series of interesting narratives. 40 cts.
BASIL, or Honesty and Industry. A capital story for boys. 35 cts.
THE HAPPY FIRESIDE. Pleasing glimpses of home life. 30 cts.
A FATHER'S LETTERS TO HIS DAUGHTER. By Gilbert West, Esq. Of great interest and value. 30 cts.
WEE DAVIE. By Rev. Dr. Norman McLeod. 30 cts.
BERTHA ALLSTON, or the Good Step-mother. 30 cts.

VERY LARGELY ILLUSTRATED VOLUMES.

FLOWERS OF SPRING-TIME. Quarto. Combining great beauty and interest, and of permanent value. $2 50.

HOME SCENES, with splendid photographic pictures. $3; morocco $5.

VIEWS FROM NATURE. A new edition, with forty engravings in tint. 90 cts.

LULLABIES, DITTIES, AND POETIC TALES FOR THE LITTLE ONES. 60 cts.

SONGS FOR THE LITTLE ONES AT HOME. A new edition. 60 cts

HOME PICTURES. With seventy fine cuts. 30 cts.

FIRESIDE PICTURES, and MY PICTURE-BOOK, with a cut on each page. Each 25 cts.

LIBRARIES FOR THE FAMILY AND SABBATH-SCHOOL.

LIFE ILLUSTRATED LIBRARY. Eighty volumes, with 275 fine engravings. $25.

THE YOUTH'S LIBRARY. Seventy volumes, with 255 Frontispieces and other Engravings. $18.

YOUNG PEOPLE'S LIBRARY. Thirty choice and finely illustrated volumes. In a case. $9.

YOUTH'S CABINET. Seventy-six volumes, largely illustrated. In a case. $9.

YOUTH'S GEMS. Sixty-four stories in 32 volumes, with beautiful engravings. With case. $4.

CHILDREN'S LIBRARY. One hundred stories in fifty volumes, many fine cuts. With case. $4.

LITTLE CHILDREN'S LIBRARY. Twenty-four books very largely illustrated. In a case, $2.

GALLAUDET'S YOUTH'S SCRIPTURE BIOGRAPHY. Eleven volumes, with fine engravings. In a case, $4.

YOUTH'S BIBLE STUDIES. In six volumes, 175 engravings. With case, $2 50.

HANNAH MORE'S STORIES FOR THE YOUNG. Eight volumes. 52 cuts. In a case, $2 50.

STORY TRUTHS. Four volumes, in a case, with beautiful cuts. $1 50.

HYMNS AND MUSIC.

SONGS OF ZION, new enlarged edition. A very choice selection of 179 chaste and popular tunes, with over 400 of the best hymns for social and family worship. 60 cts.

HAPPY VOICES. Hymns and Tunes. The children's favorite at home and in the Sabbath-school. By the hundred, $30 in stiff paper; or $35 in boards.

HYMNS FOR SOCIAL WORSHIP. Comprising 549 evangelical and devotional hymns for the social circle, the family, and the closet. Cloth, 45 cts.; sheep, 60 cts.

GEMS FOR THE PRAYER-MEETING. A beautiful pocket collection of Hymns and Music. Boards, 8 cts.; flexible cloth, 15 cts.

THE AMERICAN MESSENGER,

A monthly newspaper at 25 cents a year, five copies to one address $1, twenty copies $3 50, forty copies $6. Contains announcement of new publications.

THE BOTSCHAFTER,

Or, Messenger in German; terms the same as the American Messenger.

THE CHILD'S PAPER,

Beautifully illustrated, at eight copies for $1, forty copies $5, one hundred copies $12.

THE ILLUSTRATED FAMILY CHRISTIAN ALMANAC,

Price, 10 cents single, $1 per dozen, $7 per hundred, $60 per thousand. Postage *two cents each* to all parts of the country.

The Eclipse figured first on page 2 of the cover begins at 2h. 8.4m. mo., Washington time, in long. 297° 54'.4 W. of Washington, lat. 12° 42'.6 N. It becomes central first at 3h. 28m. mo., in long. 315° 17'.1, W., lat. 33° 32'.5 N. The annular and central Eclipse will occur at noon, at 5h. 4.8m. mo., in long. 253° 18'.1 W., lat. 48° 29'.5 N. The central Eclipse ends on the Earth at 5h. 48.4m. mo., in long. 188° 2'.8 W., lat. 67° 17'.6 N. The Eclipse leaves the Earth at 7h. 8m. mo., in long. 200° 12'.7 W., lat. 46° 48'.6 N. The Eclipse is partial in the shaded part of the engraving.

The second Eclipse illustrated on page 2 of the cover begins at 5h. 44.8m. mo., in long. 353° 26'.4 W. of Washington, lat. 14° 57'.4 S. The central Eclipse begins at noon, at 8h. 28.9m. mo., in long. 7° 55'.6 W., lat. 36° 17'.8 S. It will be central and total at noon, at 8h. 28.9m. mo., Washington time, in long. 307° 1'.2 W., lat. 46° 39'.3 S. The central and total ends on the Earth at 9h. 8.7m. mo., in long. 249° 52'.2 W., lat. 67° 3'.2 S. The Eclipse leaves the Earth at 10h. 24.5m. mo., in long. 255° 54'.2 W., lat. 46° 29'.1 S. This is the last contact. The Eclipse is partial in the darkened portion of the engraving.

LUNAR ECLIPSE. MARCH 29.

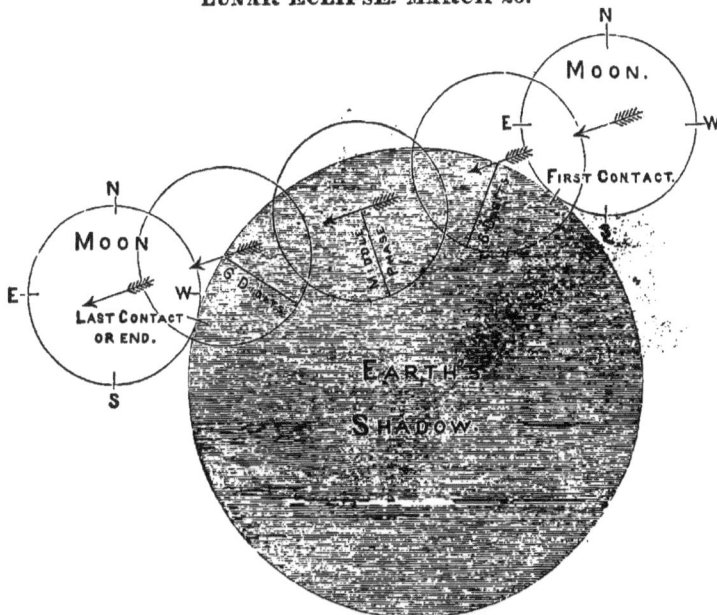

The Moon passes through the northern part of the shadow towards the east, and will be partially eclipsed on the southern limb. The Eclipse begins at the instant of first contact, which point will be 142° from the north point of the Moon towards the east. The last contact will be 106° towards the west. Greatest size, 9.756 digits. A line from the centre of the Moon to the North Star runs through the north part of the Moon.

DISTANCE OF THE FIXED STARS.—It has been commonly supposed that the most brilliant stars, of the first and second magnitude, were the nearest stars to us; but this is by no means certain. Mr. Krüger of Bonn has been observing two stars of the ninth magnitude, whose parallax, if accurately observed, proves them to be nearer to us than Arcturus, the Pole-star, or even Sirius.

A NEW STAR of about the third magnitude has suddenly appeared in the constellation of the Northern Crown, being observed in May, 1866, at Hartford, Conn., and at Cambridge, Mass. Prof. Gould says that the only known instance fairly comparable with this is the new star of 1670, which appeared suddenly as a star of the third magnitude, disappeared, shone out once more, and after two years became invisible, and has remained so since.

MEMORANDA FOR 1867.

JAN. 1. Circum.; 6, Epiph.; 13, 1st S. aft. Epiph.; 20, 2d S. aft. Epiph.; 25, Conv. of St. Paul; 27, 3d S. aft. Epiph. FEB. 2, Purif. of Virgin' Mary; 3, 4th S. aft. Epiph.; 10, 5th S. aft. Epiph; 17, Septuagesima; 24, Sexagesima and St. Matthias. MARCH 3, Quinquagesima; 6, Ash-Wednesday; 10, 1st S. in Lent; 17, 2d S. in.Lent; 24, 3d S. in Lent; 25, Annun. of Virgin Mary; 31, 4th S. in Lent. APRIL 7, 5th S. in Lent; 14, S. bef. Easter; 15, Mon. bef. Easter; 16, Tues. bef. Easter; 17, Wed. bef. Easter; 18, Thurs. bef. Easter; 19, Good-Friday; 20, Easter-even; 21, Easter-day; 22, Mon. in Easter week; 23, Tues. in Easter week; 25, St. Mark; 28, 1st S. aft. Easter. MAY 1, Sts. Philip and James; 5. 2d S. aft. Easter; 12, 3d S. aft. Easter; 19, 4th S. aft. Easter; 26. 5th S. aft. Easter; 30. Ascension-day. JUNE 2, S. aft. Ascension; 9, Whit-Sunday; 10, Mon. in Whitsun-week; 11, Tues. in Whitsun-week and St. Barnabas; 16, Trinity Sunday; 23, 1st S. aft. Trinity; 24, Nativ. of St. John Baptist; 29, St. Peter; 30, 2d S. aft. Trin. JULY 7, 3d S. aft. Trin.; 14, 4th S. aft. Trin.; 21, 5th S. aft. Trin.; 25, St James; 28, 6th S. aft. Trin. AUG. 4, 7th S. aft. Trin.; 11, 8th S. aft. Trin.; 18, 9th S. aft. Trin.; 24, St. Bartholomew; 25, 10th S. aft. Trin. SEPT. 1, 11th S. aft. Trin.; 8, 12th S. aft. Trin.; 15, 13th S. aft. Trin.; 21, St. Matthew; 22, 14th S. aft. Trin.; 29, St. Michael and All-Angels, and 15th S. aft. Trin. OCT. 6. 16th S. aft. Trin.; 13, 17th S. aft. Trin.; 18, St. Luke; 20, 18th S. aft. Trin.; 27, 19th S. aft. Trin.; 28, Sts. Simon and Jude. Nov. 1, All-Saints; 3, 20th S. aft. Trin.; 10, 21st S. aft. Trin.; 17, 22d S. aft. Trin.; 24, 23d S. aft. Trin.; 30, St. Andrew. DEC. 1, Advent Sunday; 8, 2d S. in Advent; 15, 3d S. in Advent; 21, St. Thomas; 22, 4th S. in Advent; 25, Christmas· 26, St. Stephen; 27, St. John Evan.; 28, Holy Innocents; 29, 1st S. aft. Christmas.

RATES OF POSTAGE.

Letters, prepaid by stamps, 3 cts each ½ oz. or fraction thereof, to all parts of the country, including California. If the stamp is omitted, the letter is forwarded to the Dea -letter office, and returned to the writer. *Drop* or *local* letters, 2 cts. each ½ oz. prepaid, and all letters and papers delivered in cities free of charge. *Circulars*, unsealed, 2 cts. for every three circulars to one address.

Newspapers to any part of the United States, to regular subscribers, payable quarterly in advance, *weekly*, not over 4 oz., 5 cts. a quarter, and 5 cts. for each additional 4 oz.; and an additional 5 cts. for each additional issue. *dailies* six times a week being 30 cts. a quarter. *All other regular periodicals sent to subscribers*, 1 ct. for less than 4 oz. Weekly newspapers free in the county where issued. Small periodicals referred to the Post-master General.

Books, not over 4 oz. 4 cts.; and 4 cts. for each additional 4 oz. or fraction thereof: prepaid. *Other miscellaneous packages*, not over 4 oz., 2 cts., and 2 cts. for each additional 4 oz. prepaid. These unbound miscellaneous packages include *single transient papers*, proofs, *manuscripts for books*, cards, samples, cuttings, roots, and all similar articles allowed in the mails.

FOREIGN POSTAGE. The following are the rates of postage on letters to foreign countries for each half ounce: To England, Ireland, and Scotland, 24 cts.; to France and Algeria by French mails, 15 cts. quarter ounce. By the Bremen or Hamburg mails the postage to Bremen and Hamburg is 10 cts.; to Frankfort and Wurtemburg. 15 cts.; to the German states, Prussia, Austria, and its states, and Lombardy, 15 cts.; to the Sardinian states, 23 cts.; to Papal states, 28 cts.; to the Two Sicilies, 22 cts.; to Denmark, 20 cts.; to Sweden, 33 cts.; to Norway, 38 cts.; to Russia, 29 cts. By the Prussian closed mails, or by French mail, the postage to these countries is higher. The prepayment of letters to them, excepting to the Two Sicilies, is optional; as also to Canada and the British North American states, where the postage is 10 cents under 3,000 miles, and 15 cents over. To the following, postage must be prepaid : To British West Indies, Aspinwall, Panama, and Mexico, 10 cts. under 2,500 miles. 20 cts. over; to New Granada, 18 cts.; to Peru, 22 cts.; to Ecuador, Bolivia, and Chili, 34 cts.; to Sandwich Islands, New South Wales, and China, by mail to San Francisco, thence by private ship, 10 cts.; to China and Australia via England, 33 and 45 cts., via Marseilles, 35 and 57 cents.

THE CHRISTIAN ALMANAC,
AND OTHER PUBLICATIONS OF THE AMERICAN TRACT SOCIETY,

MAY BE HAD AT 150 NASSAU-STREET, NEW YORK, S. W STEBBINS, DEPOSITARY.

BOSTON, 40 Cornhill, N. P. KEMP, Treasurer.
ROCHESTER, N. Y., 75 State-st., O. D. GROSVENOR, Agent.
PHILADELPHIA, 1210 Chestnut-st., H. N. THISSELL, Agent.
BALTIMORE, Maryland Branch, 73 W. Fayette-st., Rev. S. GUITEAU, Secretary.
CINCINNATI, Walnut-st. near Fourth. SEELY WOOD. Agent.
ST. LOUIS, 9 South-Fifth-st., J. W. MCINTYRE, Depositary.
CHICAGO, 170 South-Clark-street, C. M. HOWARD, Agent. W. G. HOLMES, Depository.
Also for sale by booksellers in the principal cities and towns.

☞ The ALMANAC is furnished at a low price to those who order it by the 100 or 1.000. The Board of the American Tract Society embraces members of fourteen evangelical denominations, united to diffuse the knowledge of Christ and him crucified by its publications, associated with personal Christian effort, at home and abroad. A donation of $20 constitutes a Life Member; $50 a Life Director.

WILLIAM A. HALLOCK. O. EASTMAN. and J. M. STEVENSON, Corresponding Sec's.
O. R. KINGSBURY, Assist. Treas., 150 Nassau-street, New York.